Be Extraordinary

Jennifer Wild

7 Key Skills to Transform Your Life

from Ordinary to Extraordinary

ROBINSON

ROBINSON

First published in Great Britain in 2020 by Robinson

1 3 5 7 9 10 8 6 4 2

A CIP catalogue record for this book is available from the British Library

ISBN: 978-1-47212-027-4

Typeset in Gentium Basic by Hewer Text UK Ltd, Edinburgh
Printed and bound in Great Britain by Clays Ltd, Elcograf S.p.A.

Papers used by Robinson are from well-managed forests and other responsible sources.

Robinson
An imprint of
Little, Brown Book Group
Carmelite House
50 Victoria Embankment
London EC4Y 0DZ

An Hachette UK Company
www.hachette.co.uk

www.littlebrown.co.uk

Dr Jennifer Wild is a consultant clinical psychologist and associate professor at the University of Oxford. She is an international expert on how to build resilience to stress and trauma, and on how to overcome post-traumatic stress disorder. She has advised the Cabinet Office on how to improve resilience in people who will face trauma in their work. She has developed and evaluated a science-informed resilience intervention for police, firefighters, paramedics and search and rescue personnel, which is being rolled out to services across England. Dr Wild regularly appears in the media giving expert advice on how to build resilience to severe stress. The documentary *Vertigo Road Trip*, in which she treats five people to overcome anxiety and lead extraordinary lives, aired on BBC One, attracting 2.2 million viewers. She has successfully helped hundreds of people to reclaim and transform their lives.

For Patricia Minden

Contents

Introduction

Some people can get over anything. Doctors diagnose them with a rare form of cancer, and they recover. They help someone in distress, are viciously attacked and blinded, yet pull through to start a successful business improving other people's lives. They are killed in combat, are miraculously brought back to life, and campaign across the country to raise awareness about the emotional difficulties linked to combat service. These people bounce back from horrendous trauma that would emotionally and physically cripple most people. They flourish with renewed resolve to face any problem with grace and ease.

We feel inspired knowing how other people achieve success in circumstances more challenging than our own. Their stories feed our curiosity about the transformational journeys of other people's lives. Yet we are often left wondering how they did it and how we could achieve success in our own lives.

Knowing how people in challenging circumstances transition from ordinary to extraordinary gives us the knowledge to transform our own lives *without* first suffering trauma.

I wrote *Be Extraordinary* while I was also being consulted as an international trauma expert to give advice on how to prevent post-traumatic stress disorder (PTSD) amongst the trapped Chilean miners, the survivors of the Boston bombings and the boys rescued from the Tham Luang Cave in Thailand.

As a psychologist, I specialise in helping people to overcome PTSD, the crippling stress reaction that afflicts soldiers and other survivors of horrific events, such as mining disasters, car crashes and the sudden death of loved ones. As a scientist, I develop and test strategies to prevent PTSD. I have built programmes based on the latest science to improve resilience for people in the most stressful and dangerous jobs, such as police officers, firefighters, paramedics and search-and-rescue personnel.

In my twenty years of practice, I have noticed something remarkable: overcoming adversity and becoming extraordinary tap the same processes. People who flourish with or without trauma as their catalyst naturally draw on seven key processes.

Informed by my own research, clinical practice and new scientific findings, in this book I reveal a life-changing formula that will lead us on the path to being extraordinary even when we encounter setbacks along the way.

We can be extraordinary

We don't need to suffer trauma to become extraordinary. We can transform our lives now. Here you'll discover the tools to be extraordinary without a traumatic catalyst. This is a book about what the tools are, how to get them and why they work.

Drawing on cognitive behavioural science, you'll discover how success is linked to changing key thinking processes and behaviours that are keeping you stuck in a rut. The same processes that keep PTSD in place keep people stuck in their own lives.

We are all going to face setbacks in our lives, whether it is a relationship break-up, loss of opportunity at work or even job loss, divorce or the death of a loved one. This is the book to read to remind us that, like the people who transformed their own tragedies into opportunities, we too can lead extraordinary lives.

In the next chapters, I reveal a human road map for change where we'll see how to adjust thoughts and behaviours that are keeping us stuck to the past, a journey that changes our focus from frustrations, setbacks or tragedy to fully engaging in the life we dream of leading, a journey that wakes us up and inspires us to grow. I will outline how to make the choices to move forward rather than staying tuned to the past, and how to overcome unhelpful processes, such as dwelling, avoidance, catastrophising, distracted attention, negative images and outdated memories, which can keep us stuck in a loop.

Each chapter includes compelling examples of ordinary people who have successfully applied these principles to their own lives to transform tragedy into extraordinary opportunity.

The 7 Key Skills

The seven key skills that will guide you to transition from ordinary to extraordinary, which also transform PTSD, are:

Vision

Vision refers to the pictures we hold in our mind's eye or the impression we have of ourselves, and our big picture for our lives. People who transition from ordinary to extraordinary prep their path to success with imagery. They transform the images that hold them back and they create winning images. But it is not just the images they hold that are vital to leading an extraordinary life, it is also the big-picture image they create for their lives. People who recover from PTSD also tap the process of Vision; they transform painful images of their trauma, their impression of feeling different to other people, and they too, in their first session of treatment, will create a vision, a plan of how they want their life to be.

In the chapter on Vision, we'll first discover how to spot and transform unhelpful images and impressions of self-doubt. Then we'll create winning images to support extraordinary success. We'll discover why transitioning from ordinary to extraordinary requires a five- and ten-year plan, and how to map a plan and keep to it when the going gets tough.

Fluid Memory

People who transition from ordinary to extraordinary clean up messy memories. No matter what they live through, they create a meaningful relationship to their past that ensures an extraordinary future. This means creating fluid memories, so we're not interrupted throughout the day by intrusive memories. And it means learning to unhook the present from past events that fuel self-doubt. People recovering from PTSD also transform their memories, connecting new information to their most troublesome moments, smoothing their memories and making them less threatening.

In the chapter on Fluid Memory, we'll transform our everyday stressors and difficult memories, so they motivate rather than defeat us, and we'll discover how to unhook the present from past events that fuel self-doubt.

Focus

People who transition from ordinary to extraordinary with or without trauma as their catalyst choose to focus on what they can do rather than on what they can't or on what may be lost to the past. They also develop their attention muscle since they realise that time could well be limited. These people optimise their minutes by focusing efficiently without distraction. People who have got through the other side of a trauma and are recovering from PTSD also learn to shift their focus – away from their fears and on to what is going on in the here and now, which increases their sense of safety.

In the chapter on Focus, we'll look at helpful and unhelpful attention. We'll also discover how to strengthen our attention muscle, a much-needed skill to thrive.

Helpful Thinking Habits

Part of the training to think like a winner is to recognise unhelpful habits, such as dwelling and catastrophising, and to transform them. We need to develop healthy thinking habits too that tap proactive language and guide you to interpret ambiguity or uncertainty in positive ways. Healthy thinking, like happiness, can be trained. It's a skill we can learn. When people overcome PTSD, the thinking habit they most often transform is emotional reasoning, using feelings, rather than facts, to guide thinking and decision-making. In PTSD, the feeling is most often one of fear, and when people feel afraid, they believe with the same intensity that something bad will happen. This is emotional reasoning – linking the likelihood of an outcome to the intensity of a feeling.

The chapter on Helpful Thinking Habits reveals the most effective tips for noticing unhelpful thinking processes and how to nip them in the bud, so they don't spiral out of control. Here, you'll discover the 'Thinking Gym', which gives exercises on how to develop responsible language, how to transform 'why' thinking into 'how' thinking, and how to think in shades of colour rather than in black and white.

Extraordinary Behaviours

Avoidance is the number-one behaviour that keeps people stuck in a rut. It is also the number-one behaviour that keeps PTSD going. But four extraordinary behaviours pave the path to success: exercise, sound sleep, planning ahead and compassion.

In the chapter on Extraordinary Behaviours, I'll take you through nine scientifically proven ways to overcome avoidance and the four key behaviours to keep you on your extraordinary track. You'll discover what they are, the science behind them and how to incorporate them into your life.

Determination

Determination is the inner grit that keeps you going on your worthy projects and meaningful goals. People who transition from ordinary to extraordinary are motivated to start and determined to keep going. They maintain momentum on their path to success like people who overcome PTSD, determined to overcome negative circumstances and build a better life.

In the chapter on Determination, we'll look at how to maintain your momentum on your path to success. We'll learn the difference between determination and motivation. You'll discover how to pick up momentum and run with your big vision, even in the face of defeat.

Cultivating Happiness

Cultivating happiness encapsulates choices to be happy. Happiness, like an attitude, is a mindset we cultivate. Overcoming trauma or transitioning from ordinary to extraordinary requires the capacity to overcome everyday losses and offers the opportunity to tap tools to feel upbeat and happy on the path to extraordinary success.

In the chapter on Cultivating Happiness, we'll discover how to deal with everyday losses in our own lives and learn the tools to keep us upbeat and happy on our path to extraordinary success.

The 7 Extraordinary People

The seven extraordinary people who feature in this book include three individuals I have worked with on their recovery from PTSD and four remarkable individuals I have interviewed from around the world, who have transitioned from ordinary to extraordinary. They range in age from twenty-four to seventy-four and are of different ethnicities and gender. They provide compelling examples of how the processes can be used even in the most difficult of times.

Kenny

Brutally attacked on a London bus whilst helping a pregnant woman, Kenny's act of kindness cost him his sight. He developed, then recovered from, PTSD and is now a thriving personal trainer, guiding people with and without disabilities to achieve their best possible physical fitness. He has also started a business supplying shea butter to English skincare firms, and is leading a grassroots project in Ghana to build a sustainable student hostel for the local university.

Kenny exemplifies the process of Vision, having learned to replace images of what he looked like after his attack with more positive ones and having created, then followed, the bigger vision for his life.

Joshua

A twenty-four-year-old American soldier who was shot and killed whilst on a humanitarian aid mission in Iraq, Joshua was miraculously revived then went on to successfully appeal US Congress to increase funds for US troops to support their emotional recovery from combat, working with CNN, Fox TV, ABC and the *New York Times* in the process. He is now a major contributor to the Wounded Warriors Project, a charitable organisation in the USA dedicated to helping veterans recover physically and emotionally from their combat service.

Joshua best illustrates the process of Fluid Memory. He updated his memory of himself, with effort, from being a fit soldier on duty to being killed and weakened and to being a soldier who survived with a wealth of knowledge and experience to help other soldiers deal with the emotional stress of combat.

Mary

A white English woman who converted from Catholicism to Islam in her twenties after her brother died by suicide, Mary lovingly raised four children while ignoring her health, only to discover that a lump in her breast had grown to 10 cm in size within a year. She was whisked into surgery where a radical mastectomy was performed. Against all odds, Mary recovered physically and emotionally. Delving deep into her experience, she went on to empower other people through their journeys with cancer.

Mary best exemplifies the process of Focus. She regularly shifted her attention out of her head to feel confident after the surgery that radically changed her body, and she trained to focus efficiently to develop a programme to care for men and women newly diagnosed with cancer.

Joyce

In the 1950s, Joyce was a junior doctor with ambitions to become a consultant. At the age of fifty-one, she developed a rare form of blood cancer. She pulled through and was cancer-free for fifteen years. But it came back when she was sixty-eight years old. She was treated with a new drug in a medical study and was the only one to recover. At the age of seventy-five, Joyce recovered from her second bout of cancer and retrained as a psychotherapist to counsel young men with schizophrenia.

Joyce best demonstrates Helpful Thinking Habits. She dealt with numerous bouts of dwelling when the cancer came back, and she beat catastrophising symptoms of ill health when she noticed them.

Caroline

Born into a regular, middle-class family in France, Caroline got hooked on heroin in her teens. She quit by herself and is now a well-respected nurse pioneering new healthcare programmes for bereaved children in Cambodia.

There is no doubt Caroline best represents Extraordinary Behaviours, demonstrating how to overcome avoidance for good and kick-start healthy behaviours to pave the path to extraordinary success.

Charlotte

An American woman born into upper-middle-class wealth, Charlotte suffered setback after setback, including early separation from her parents and life-threatening illness as a teenager. She turned her life around, graduated from an Ivy League university as a mature student and was pursuing a career in Russian Languages when her grandfather became gravely ill. She gave up her career, moved overseas to care for him, wrote and sold film scripts, directed one, which won a prestigious award, but was unsuccessful in securing funds to produce her most passionate project, a romantic comedy. After ten years of trying, she left the film industry and returned to university to study clinical pharmacology. Upon graduating she started a successful bioscience company and is now funding her romantic comedy with the profits from her business.

Having endured and bounced back from repeated setbacks on her path to enormous success, without a doubt, Charlotte best captures the process of Determination.

Afet

An energetic young woman who lost her legs, much of her hearing and the capacity to have children after a medical misdiagnosis, Afet is now an enthusiastic caterer, creating scrumptious occasions for her clients, a fresh force in the world, and an inspiration to those she meets. Afet transformed enormous losses on her road to success, choosing happiness daily.

As we discover the tools to tap happiness in our own lives and how to overcome everyday losses, we'll learn from Afet who best illustrates the process of Cultivating Happiness.

How to use this book

Each chapter explains one of the seven processes that transition people from ordinary to extraordinary and shows people who used the processes on their own paths to success. The chapters include key exercises, questions and, where relevant, details of online tools that will help you to practise these processes in your own life.

I suggest you have a journal to hand as you work through *Be Extraordinary* where you can jot notes and answers to questions. Or you could create an electronic document to type notes and answers.

Some people might prefer to work through the book with a group of friends or colleagues where they talk through the chapters, share stories and keep the momentum going while also enjoying the process.

However you choose to use *Be Extraordinary*, you will find that the chapters inspire extraordinary thinking, extraordinary possibilities for success and provide practical steps with the scientifically proven strategies for creating a life that matches your dreams rather than your self-doubts.

Be Extraordinary has the potential to create and inspire extraordinary change in our lives, readying you to better face bumps that may appear on your road to success. Like happiness, being extraordinary causes a ripple effect, inspiring the people around you. Extraordinary success for you means extraordinary inspiration for the people close to you and extraordinary progress for our wider community in overcoming the challenges we face. Seize the opportunity to create an extraordinary life. You don't have to suffer a trauma to be extraordinary. You can be extraordinary now.

I.

Vision

On 4 August 2012, Jessica Ennis ran her final event of the heptathlon in London's summer Olympic Games. Eighty thousand people cheek by jowl in the stadium, tense on their feet, tears streaming, roared with cheers every stride of her 800-metre race. She crossed the finish line in a breathless two minutes and eight seconds, breaking British records and winning Olympic gold. It was an unforgettable moment.

When we watch elite athletes excel, achieve world records, score goals with seconds to spare or smash their personal bests, we wonder how they do it. We know they work hard, dedicate their lives to sport, practise for years and top up with the best nutrition and coaches. But what makes one athlete outperform another when it really counts?

Jessica Ennis-Hill says she perfects her performance with images: she creates the perfect image of succeeding in her mind's eye. She believes it affects her physical performance. And it does. Science has shown that picturing a technique in imagery strengthens the neural firings in the muscles that matter and creates what feels like a real experience for the brain, honing skills and sharpening performance.

Wayne Rooney, one of the UK's top footballers, uses imagery in the run-up to matches, picturing himself scoring goals over and over, especially the night before a game. Jonny Wilkinson, possibly the world's best rugby player, now retired, would imagine how the ball would feel when it hit his foot, and the trajectory it would travel once he had kicked it that would take it through to a goal. Wimbledon champions Andy Murray and Novak Djokovic prime their play with imagery.

These elite athletes top up their training with images. Their vivid imagery practice is as important to their success as their practice on the court, the pitch or the track. It helps their minds to prepare mentally, improves their confidence, their focus and their muscle memories. It helps them to outperform under pressure. These athletes create winning images. And they win. Their images are vivid, detailed and in real time.

Like elite athletes, people who transition from ordinary to extraordinary prep their path to success with imagery. They transform the images that hold them back and they create winning images.

In this chapter we'll look at how to transform unhelpful images and how to create winning ones. We'll learn from Kenny, who lost his vision helping a stranger on a London bus. Kenny recovered from his attack, regained 25 per cent of his vision and is now a thriving personal trainer with a passion for helping communities in Africa to build eco-friendly student hostels. Having lost most of his eyesight, how Kenny processed information changed. He began to think in vivid, clear pictures – images that transformed his misfortune to success.

Here we'll create our own thriving images and we'll learn why transitioning from ordinary to extraordinary requires a five- and ten-year plan. Importantly, we'll discover how to map a plan and keep to it when the going gets tough.

1. The Power of Negative Images

Why is a picture more powerful than a thought?

Imagine drifting to sleep late in the night when suddenly you hear an unusual rustling or a muffled creaking. What is it? Your mind races. Perhaps it's a floorboard creaking or a cupboard closing. Your heart speeds up as you picture a thug making his way through the corridor to your very room. Your hands sweat and you feel terrified.

Imagine the same scenario again. But this time, when you hear the unusual rustling or floorboard creaking, you picture your quirky tabby cat trotting from one room to the next, wide awake in her nocturnal explorations. You chuckle, picture her inquisitive face, then snuggle into the covers as you slip into sleep.

The images here differ completely and lead to entirely different feelings. One image leads to full-blown fear and the other leads to so much calm, you fall asleep.

Of course, when you hear the rustling, instead of thinking in images, you could say to yourself: 'It could be a stranger in the house.' Or: 'It could be my cat.' The thoughts will increase or decrease anxiety a bit, but they're much less likely to create full-on-fear or Zen-like calm.

Images are compelling. Like pictures, they tell whole stories. They affect how we feel, how we behave, how we perform and even how people see us. In one study, psychologist Colette Hirsch and her team at King's College London told people to bring to mind a negative image of themselves – such as seeing themselves stumbling over words and trembling as they tried to speak – and then to have a conversation with a stranger. Once the conversation was over, they asked them to create in their mind's eye a positive picture of themselves – such as speaking with ease and looking confident – and to hold it in mind in a second conversation.

They told other people to conjure up a positive image in their first conversation and then a negative one in their second conversation. The psychologists video-recorded the conversations and then had another person rate their performance.

> Images affect how we feel, behave, perform and even how people see us.

They discovered something fascinating: whenever people pictured a negative image of themselves, whether it was in the first or second conversation, they always felt and performed worse than when they held a positive image in mind. The person rating the conversations, who had no idea what image each person was holding in their mind, rated people as coming across much worse when they held a negative rather than a positive image in mind.

What this tells us is that the pictures we hold in our mind's eye matter. They have the power to strengthen our path to extraordinary success, or to keep us spinning the wheel of self-doubt and mediocrity. At worst, they can cause a lot of distress and anxiety.

Does everyone have images?

The short answer is yes – we all have images or impressions of ourselves.

Some people are more visual in their thinking and their images will be pictures that come to mind. Other people will have an *impression* in different situations: a sense of stuffing up or a sense of nailing it. Since imagery includes impressions and most people have a sense of how they are coming across or a sense of their capacity for success, it's safe to say that most people will have images. But we're often unaware of them even when we face a setback like being passed over for promotion, where we're more likely to question our own impressions for success.

In these moments, our impressions or images of ourselves give clues about niggling self-doubts. It is these niggling self-doubts that need to go because they determine how you interpret the successes in your life, and whether or not you'll quickly pick yourself up and dust yourself off when you face a hiccup on your path to being extraordinary.

People transitioning from ordinary to extraordinary use images to their advantage: they go out of their way to create winning pictures and they direct attention away from feelings of doubt towards their best possible outcomes captured in their images.

How do negative images keep people stuck?

Negative images cause a lot of problems. The main one is that people tend to believe their images and impressions, whether they're picturing being attacked in the middle of the night or sensing they're stumbling over words in a speech. While the image is in mind, it feels like their worst fears will happen, and this keeps anxiety and other awful feelings intact. But this is not the only problem.

Negative images push people to use what we call *safety-seeking behaviours* – these are behaviours we're inclined to use to feel safe, but which actually keep our attention on our worst fears, making them feel like they're more likely to happen.

For example, if you have an image of stumbling over your words in a presentation with beads of sweat running down your forehead, you'll be more inclined to avoid eye contact, try to cover up the parts of your body you're worried will sweat, and continually monitor in your mind's eye how well you're coming across. While you're doing all this checking, your attention is stuck to your worst fears and has turned away from the task at hand. While you're monitoring yourself, trying to come across well and prevent your worst fears from happening, you are much more likely to lose your train of thought and actually stumble over words. You'll also be more attuned to sensations of sweating, which will make you feel like it's more noticeable than it really is.

Negative images also make it harder to make sense of common cues. When we have a negative image of being attacked we're much less likely to interpret the unfamiliar sound as harmless. If we hold an image of ourselves looking like a gibbering wreck, we'll be much less likely to see someone's smile as encouraging. We'll be more inclined to misinterpret their smile as a sign that they're laughing at us.

Finally, negative images make it easier to remember matching memories, which means we're more likely to conclude that what we're worried about is really going to happen. Our brain will be accessing the few times our worry came true rather than the many times it didn't. So, if you hear that noise in the night and imagine a thug making his way through your house to attack you, while this image is in mind, you'll be more likely to remember the times you've seen this on TV or heard about it happening, rather than the many times you've heard a similar noise with nothing drastic following.

The underlying meaning of negative images

Behind the negative images are highly charged thoughts such as 'A thug is going to kill me' or 'I'll come across as incompetent in the presentation'. And behind the thoughts lies a deeper meaning. The thoughts and the underlying meaning drive behaviour. If the image is negative, the thoughts and underlying meaning keep people stuck in a rut. When the images and linked thoughts are positive, they support extraordinary success.

Once my clients and I have spotted their negative images and the thoughts behind them, I work to uncover the worst meaning. The worst meaning is our source of doubt, indecision and the fodder for future negative images. Change the worst meaning and we can create successful images much more swiftly.

2. Overcoming Negative Images that Hold You Back

How do we change a limiting image?

First things first. First we have to spot our most problematic image or impression, discover the underlying meaning and update it.

The best way to spot a problematic image or impression is to think of a recent situation where you felt anxious, such as a job interview, a meeting with a difficult colleague, a time when you were caught up in traffic and were late for an important meeting or a time when you were asked to speak in public.

If you cannot think of a situation where you felt some anxiety, call to mind a setback you've faced where you felt disappointed, such as being passed over for promotion, performing less than your best in an interview or talk or pitching an idea to your CEO that she swiftly rejected.

Close your eyes and recreate the scene as vividly as possible. Picture where you were and who you were with. Talk yourself through the detail in the present tense as if it's happening now and you're a film director who is about to capture it all on camera.

Paint a detailed picture in your mind's eye. What can you **see** and **hear**? What do you feel in **your body**? Are **other people** in your image? What are they doing? What do you notice about them? What is **your feeling** about what is happening and about what you think is going to happen? If your anxious situation is a job interview or other social event, describe the feeling you have about how you're coming across, and the feeling you have about how others are responding to you. Capture the picture in as much detail as possible. See the image vividly. Then answer these two important questions: **What is the worst thing about the image or impression? What does it say about you as a person?**

One of my clients, Carina, described feeling nervous in a meeting with her boss where she was asked about the progress of her project. She remembered **seeing** her hands fidgeting on her lap, and her boss (**other person**) frowning, **hearing** herself speaking softly, **feeling** hot in the face (**body sensation**), and **feeling** self-conscious and shaky. She had an impression that she was coming across as awkward and unprepared and that her boss was disappointed in her. When I asked what the worst thing was about her impression, she said that it meant she was a nervous wreck who would never succeed at her job. When I asked what the impression meant about her as a person, she said that it meant she would always be jittery in meetings. 'What's so bad about this?' I asked to uncover the deeper meaning. She replied that it meant she was incompetent.

These beliefs ('I'll never succeed at my job' and 'I'm incompetent'), encapsulated in her impression, were keeping her stuck. They were the lens through which she saw her world. Whatever Carina experienced, whether it was a tough interview or an interview that led to success, her beliefs worked like a magnet, pulling details to fit them. So instead of seeing an interview as useful prep for future interviews, if Carina wasn't subsequently hired she remembered details like 'the panel frowned', 'I spoke quickly' and 'I wasn't hired' as evidence that she was incompetent.

If Carina was hired after interview, her beliefs led her to 'yes, but' the outcome, so instead of seeing herself as competent and the best candidate, she again remembered details like 'I spoke quickly', and 'the panel frowned', which led her to doubt her success with thoughts like 'I was lucky' or 'I just got through the interview'. Her beliefs filtered how she saw her success and strengthened rather than weakened the worst meaning of her impression.

To help overcome her stuck-in-a-rut impression, we updated the beliefs, then transformed her sense that she came across as awkward and incompetent by creating a new image based on facts not feelings.

Whilst Carina may have known intellectually that she was competent, she had an overriding sense that she was incompetent. She made decisions that stopped her from stretching herself and focused on details that could loosely support limiting beliefs while ignoring praise and achievements that supported empowering beliefs. She had what psychologists call a head-heart lag. Transforming her sense of competence in imagery helped her to feel and know in her heart that she was competent rather than just accepting it intellectually.

The roots of limiting images

Our most problematic impressions and images are rooted in limiting beliefs, which filter how we view our past, how we see our present and what we expect for our future. Often these beliefs originate with a specific event in the past, such as being humiliated, bullied or severely criticised. When our most troublesome image is linked to a past event, then the memory will carry the same meaning as the image.

To discover if the image or impression you've spotted is linked to a memory, ask yourself when you first remember feeling the same way as in the image. If a past event springs to mind, then your image may be a snapshot of your memory. This is not a problem at all since when our images are linked to a memory, they carry the same meaning, and to create thriving images, we're updating that limiting meaning.

This chapter will guide you to create your extraordinary belief and to feel its effects in an empowering image, which is similar to having a real experience. But you may also find it helpful to revisit the memory, if there is one, with your new belief in tow. 'How do I break the links to the past?' covers how to do this in the next chapter.

The worst meaning is your prejudice

The worst meaning of your image or impression is the prejudice you hold against yourself. We all know how resistant prejudices are to change. That's why the belief, the worst meaning, hasn't crumbled over the years. If anything, it's probably got stronger because your mind effortlessly filters everyday experiences to fit with your beliefs.

Knowing that your mind maps your experiences to fit your beliefs or, put another way, your beliefs filter how you see the world is just more reason why you've got to get on top of your beliefs to lead an extraordinary life, especially the ones lurking behind your images and impressions.

How do I update a limiting meaning?

Updating a limiting meaning is much like overcoming a prejudice. Christine Padesky, a leading expert in cognitive behavioural therapy, suggests that the key to transforming such strongly held self-critical beliefs is to treat them like a prejudice you are trying to overcome. For example, if you had a friend who believed all women were out to snare a millionaire, what steps would you take to transform their belief? Most likely your first step would be to find contradictory evidence. This may include finding a woman who is happily single and supporting herself or finding a woman in a relationship who supports her partner. You may find several women who fit this description.

Of course, if your friend firmly believed that women were out to snare a millionaire then he might conclude that your exemplar women are exceptions to the rule. You may ask your friend to make a note of every time they meet a woman who supports herself or who fully supports herself plus a family. Your friend would soon gather a lot of evidence that would no longer fit with the idea that these women are an exception to the rule.

11

You may ask your friend to count up the number of women they've come across who have snared a millionaire and to compare this with the number they've come across who work to support themselves. With this kind of evidence, you may be able to guide your friend to change their belief to something like: 'Women hold myriad ambitions. Some women may wish to snare a millionaire, but most women wish to support themselves and many women want to support themselves and their families financially.'

The key to changing your own worst meaning is to take a similar approach. First, look for contradictory evidence, make a note of evidence that disconfirms the belief and come up with a new belief that's more accurate and more likely to support success. Then make an effort to note evidence that supports your new belief.

It's like going to the gym but with much less sweat. We train our mind to tune to the signs of our new belief rather than the limiting one until it's automatic. As you'll learn in Chapter V, Extraordinary Behaviours, this can take anywhere from 18 to 264 days. 264 days may sound like a lot, but thinking about how many days the limiting belief has ruled the roost (thousands, if not tens of thousands), then the number between 8 and 264 is really just a handful of times, maybe several handfuls of times, and well worth the effort, given how your new belief will boost your mood and your success.

The sense of inadequacy

The worst meanings of our images or impressions hold a strong sense of inadequacy like 'I'm incompetent', 'I'm stupid', 'I'm vulnerable' or 'I'm unlovable'. They are often coupled with a worry that people will detect these inner failings, then reject us. The key to updating our worst meanings is to recognise the difference between how we feel and how we come across, the difference between how we feel and how we behave. We first find examples that do not fit with the idea of being incompetent, stupid, vulnerable, unlovable or other feelings of inadequacy we may have noted, then we look for evidence that shows that people accept us. If you've noted that 'I'm incompetent and stupid, other people will notice then reject me', take a moment to list achievements and then situations where you've helped people.

What are achievements?

Achievements include things you were afraid to try and did anyway, such as learning to drive, bungee jumping, becoming a parent, travelling to a foreign country on your own, hosting a party, learning to ski or snowboard, giving a presentation or other activity that challenged you. Achievements also include, of course, all the standard accomplishments like graduating with a diploma or university degree, recognising a relationship that's not working and separating, finalising a divorce, starting a business, raising a child, and so on.

I've got my achievements, now what?

Once you've made a list of your achievements, take a moment to note situations where you've been helpful, such as helping your son with his homework, helping your girlfriend fix her car, cooking a healthy lunch for your dad, typing up an agenda for your boss, giving a loving home to a pet, helping a stranger with directions, and so on.

13

Reorientate your focus

The key is to reorientate your focus: what have I achieved? Who have I helped and how? Then think hard about rejection and if it's relevant today.

We all have rejection in our past. We may have been rejected by a person we fancied or been repeatedly not chosen for various sports teams at school. We may have been teased or even bullied.

The important question to answer is: are you rejected today? What are the signs that people accept you, that they are kind and friendly to you? Call to mind invitations you've received to grab a bite to eat with friends, to go to a party, a talk, a wedding, a film or a date. Call to mind a time when a friend or family member called to ask for your opinion or advice or a time when a stranger smiled at you.

What we are doing here is linking behaviours to signs of your value rather than linking feelings of inadequacy to impressions of failure. We're aiming to shrink the gap between how you feel about yourself

14

in your worst moments and how people really see you, which they base on facts rather than your feelings. Think about how you see a close friend and how you would describe them. Then apply the appreciation you extend to others, your own capacity to notice their helpful behaviours, to yourself to re-evaluate the worst meaning linked to your image or impression. How accurate is it really?

Kenny's Story

On 13 September 2001, Kenny, twenty-three years old, caught a bus on his way home from his security work at The Gap in London. He was studying electronic engineering and had taken up part-time security work to support his girlfriend and their soon-to-be-born son. The bus was packed when he got on with his friend from work. But there were three spare seats on the top deck. He and his friend sat up there, taking up two of the free seats. There was one left next to a pregnant woman. At the next stop, a group of guys got on the bus and searched for seats. One guy started yelling at the pregnant woman with the free seat beside her because the seat was covered with crushed biscuits. Kenny tried to reason with the guy but instead this guy gathered his friends and they attacked Kenny. They gouged out his left eye and damaged his right. Passengers screamed as they saw Kenny's eye hanging from its socket on his left cheek. The bus driver fled the scene, terrified. Emergency services were quick to respond and rushed Kenny to hospital where doctors put him in an induced coma to calm the swelling in his brain and protect whatever vision he might have left.

When he woke three days later, Kenny didn't know where he was and stumbled his way to the toilet where he looked at himself in the mirror. The doctors had taped his left eye to his cheek; they were waiting for him to wake up so they could speak to him about removing it. But he woke up earlier than expected and without medical staff nearby. His first image of himself captured the aftermath of his trauma: a swollen, bruised face with his left eye hanging by its optic nerve on his face, held in place by surgical tape. Kenny became a medical experiment as doctors tried new treatments to calm the swelling in his brain and restore his vision. He was in hospital for three months. He was depressed and had daily images of screaming faces plaguing his mind.

I treated Kenny for PTSD. We worked together to transform his images. He had two types: terrifying images from the trauma, of people screaming in terror, and extreme images of how he thought he looked to other people. He pictured himself as he first saw his face in hospital, swollen and with his eye taped to his cheek. Over months, Kenny's physical appearance healed. He had a prosthetic eye and the swelling and bruises completely recovered. But he had an impression of looking grotesque and this was activated when he looked at himself in his bathroom mirror in the morning to insert his prosthetic eye and when he talked to other people.

To help Kenny overcome PTSD and to thrive, we updated the deeper beliefs captured in his images and transformed the pictures he held in his mind. Kenny is now a successful personal trainer for people with and without disabilities. He has started his own company supplying shea butter to English skincare firms and has bought land in Ghana where he is building environmentally friendly student hostels for the local university.

3. Harnessing the Power of Positive Images

Rebooting our beliefs

So here we are. You've loosened the worst meaning linked to your image or impression with evidence. It's time now to reboot your beliefs. If your worst meaning captured a sense of inadequacy, and you've chipped away the shaky ground on which this belief stood, you're equipped to build a new one. Having reviewed your evidence, it's time to ask yourself what is a more realistic belief? What can you add to your realistic belief to make it your extraordinary belief? The belief that is going to kick self-doubt and couch-potato behaviour when you're feeling less than your best? The belief that will push you to achieve rather than give in?

Looking at your list of achievements, ask yourself: what do they say about you as a person? What does this *really* mean? How will the best meaning support your future success?

For example, Carina had achieved a degree in sociology. Whilst studying full time, she had cared for her mother, coordinated her many hospital appointments and helped to keep her mum's mind active with puzzles and word games she had sourced online after reviewing research on early dementia. Carina said her achievements meant that she is bright, organised, a problem-solver, a hard worker, and a kind-hearted person with grit. She said what this really means is that she can achieve whatever she puts her mind to. In terms of future success, believing she can achieve whatever she puts her mind to gives her the confidence to take steps towards her big vision. Her path to success becomes a series of practical steps because she has cleared the beliefs holding her back.

What is your extraordinary belief?

Extraordinary beliefs keep you going when the going gets tough. They focus on facts, the best meaning of your achievements, and they include evidence: evidence of success. Including evidence of success helps to get you back on track rather than spiral towards giving up when you face a hiccup or setback in your path. Extraordinary beliefs, when wrapped with images, also include a person or people who would be most proud of your success. This is important because spotting who really supports your success helps you to tap compassion in moments of setbacks, which means you'll be more likely to problem-solve to put yourself back on your path to extraordinary rather than quitting and struggling with self-doubt.

To help build your extraordinary belief, you may first want to write out the worst meaning of your image or impression, what you've learned about the worst meaning, then tune to your achievements and what they say about you as a person. The next step is to build your belief: include facts, the best meaning of your achievements, evidence, and a person or people who would relish your success.

Sound complicated? Here are some examples.

Carina's prep for creating her extraordinary belief:

Worst meaning of image or impression	I'm jittery in meetings. I'll never succeed at my job. People will think I'm incompetent.
Learning linked to worst meaning	I feel incompetent when I focus on my feelings rather than facts. I've been looking at the world through a lens focused on signs of incompetence. I need to change the lens to spot signs of my competence.
My achievements	• Degree in sociology • Whilst studying, I cared for my mum, coordinated her hospital appointments and sourced stimulating word games shown to be helpful in early dementia • Hired by local charity to write reports
Best meaning of my achievements	I'm bright, organised, a problem-solver, hard worker and a kind person with grit. What this really means is that I can achieve whatever I put my mind to.

The nuts and bolts of Carina's extraordinary belief:

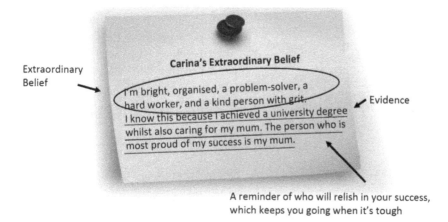

Extraordinary Belief

Carina's Extraordinary Belief

I'm bright, organised, a problem-solver, a hard worker, and a kind person with grit. I know this because I achieved a university degree whilst also caring for my mum. The person who is most proud of my success is my mum.

Evidence

A reminder of who will relish in your success, which keeps you going when it's tough

Joshua's prep for creating his extraordinary belief:

Worst meaning of image or impression	I'm incompetent and stupid, people will see this and reject me.
Learning linked to worst meaning	I'm way more acceptable than I feel. When I focus on feelings of self-doubt, I discount my achievements and miss opportunities to feel and act competently.
My achievements	• Bungee jumped in NZ even though I was terrified • Graduated with a solid degree in engineering • Wrote some code during my BSc, which my supervisor is still using • Built a basic robot, which still works today
Best meaning of my achievements	I'm organised and motivated, and I push myself even when I'm anxious. What this really means is that I can achieve my goals when I put my mind to it.

Joshua's Extraordinary Belief

I'm organised and motivated, I always achieve my goals when I put my mind to it, just like I bungee jumped through my fear of heights. The people I value (Ted, David & Amy) will be most proud of my success.

Mary's prep for creating her extraordinary belief:

Worst meaning of image or impression	I'm weak and stupid and will never reach my goals. I'll always be second best.
Learning linked to worst meaning	I feel weak and stupid when I focus on my feelings and fear of failing rather than when I focus on facts, my achievements and feedback from supervisors and employers.
My achievements	• I've raised four children • I cared for my mother who suffered with Alzheimer's • I pitched an idea to the local hospital about resources for carers and they've asked me to contribute to their website • I supported my family through my cancer diagnosis
Best meaning of my achievements	I'm innovative, creative, hard-working, proactive and strong. What this really means is that I do have what it takes.

Mary's Extraordinary Belief

I'm innovative, creative, hard-working, proactive and strong. I have what it takes. I know this because I've raised four children and supported my family through my cancer diagnosis. The people who will be most proud of my success are my children.

The next step

Now that you have your extraordinary belief, the next step is to wrap it with an image. Remember, an image is more powerful than words alone. You'll be strengthening your new belief like a muscle by linking it to an image and frequently calling that image to mind.

Wrapping the belief with an image

Sir Ranulph Fiennes was the first person to circumnavigate the world, including crossing the Artic and Antarctica, using only surface transport – an extremely challenging and dangerous expedition taking seven years of preparation and three years to undertake. He spoke recently in Oxford. When asked,

'What keeps you going when you're about to give up?' he replied, 'I picture the two people I'd feel most ashamed to let down.'

> Images that motivate extraordinary success include details of succeeding.
>
> They also include the person or people we most aspire to make proud.

In the toughest moments of his expeditions, Sir Ranulph Fiennes used images to support his success. When the pull to give up was strong, he pictured his father and his grandfather, two people he aspired to make proud and whom he had never met.

So, to get started, imagine a situation you'd like to succeed in. This could be giving a presentation, a job interview, running your first 10 km race, finishing a thesis, buying your first home or pitching your start-up to investors.

Picture yourself in the situation and picture yourself absolutely achieving it. What would that look like? What would you look like? What expression would your face convey? What would you feel? Picture yourself accomplishing the goal. Include facts. If you've given a presentation before and have seen yourself in a photo or video having accomplished this, well, you know what you look like. Include these details. Or, if you nailed a 5 km and are aiming for a 10 km race, draw on your experience of achieving a 5 km to detail accomplishing a longer race. What do you see? What do you hear?

What do you feel? Picture in your image at least one person you aspire to make proud. This could be a child, a parent, a person from childhood who supported you, a partner or a friend.

Next, check your image against your extraordinary belief. Does your image encapsulate a picture of success that matches your new belief?

If so, you've created a winning image. Whenever you feel less than your best, whenever you feel vulnerable, incompetent or some other version of inadequate, call to mind your image of you succeeding, of seeing the person or people you aspire to make most proud spurring you on.

4. How Did Kenny Do It?

Kenny had **images** of how he thought he appeared to other people. These images were snapshots of the worst moment of the trauma, when he saw himself in the hospital mirror with his left eye taped to his cheek. He had an **impression** that he looked different, that there was a pulsating bump on his forehead and that his left eye looked grotesque and damaged.

To update Kenny's images, I first helped him to see how he really looked today and that this was very different to the moment frozen in his mind of what he looked like in hospital. I asked Kenny to show me photos taken since his trauma and to compare them to his hospital photos. I also encouraged Kenny to talk to other people out and about where I took photos of him whilst talking. We compared these to the photos Kenny had of himself in hospital. Looking at the photos, it became obvious to Kenny that he looks more similar than different to other people. He could see that his left eye looked the same as his right eye and there was no longer swelling or bruising to his face. The image in his mind was out of date and reflected a moment from his trauma.

The worst meaning of Kenny's images

The worst meaning of Kenny's images tapped a sense of difference, damage and rejection. Kenny believed that he was different, defective and that people would notice then reject him.

Updating the worst meaning linked to Kenny's images

To update his belief, we first spotted his similarities to other people then looked at how accurate his thought was that he is rejected. The trauma was an extreme and violent form of rejection, but Kenny had no evidence of being rejected since. He was still with his girlfriend, they had a son, he dropped his son to school and no one refused to talk to him or excluded him in conversation when he stayed afterwards to chat to other parents. He continued to have friends.

It was important to help Kenny recognise what he was still able to do and to shift his attention from what he had lost to what had not been lost. Kenny made a list of what he was still able to do, which included being a father, being able to exercise, making his son laugh, being able to walk, run, read books in large print, enjoy music, start a business he was passionate about and make it a successful one. He realised that while he had lost quite a bit of vision, there were ways he could see. He could read in large print and he could enjoy an audio book, he could rely on hearing the world more than on seeing the world.

Kenny also made a list of his values. He valued honesty, hard work, persistence and kindness. When he focused on his values, he realised that he was more similar than different to other people. We updated the belief 'I am different, defective and

24

people will notice then reject me' to 'I am more similar than different to other people, I come across as acceptable and people are kind and friendly to me, accepting rather than rejecting me'. Kenny concluded that perhaps he was the one who had been unable to accept himself.

Kenny's extraordinary belief

Thinking about his achievements, including his trauma recovery, Kenny came up with: 'I am resourceful, strong, reliable and kind. I am more similar than different to other people. Where I may differ is in my extraordinary strength that guided me through my trauma recovery. The person I aspire to make most proud is my son.'

Wrapped with an image

The image Kenny created in his mind's eye to capture his extraordinary belief was based on a photo taken after he had pushed his first client to reach his personal best on the bench press. His client's muscular arm is wrapped around Kenny's shoulders and Kenny is smiling from cheek to cheek. In his image, Kenny's son is also hugging his leg, beaming with pride.

Kenny's next steps

When Kenny had the impression that he was coming across as defective and different, that people would reject him, he reminded himself of what he knows now: that he is more similar than different to other people, that whilst his vision had changed, he had not lost his ability to experience the world, to be a father, to exercise, to create and follow his passion, to read with audio books, and to hear and feel much more of his experiences. He called to mind his extraordinary belief.

Kenny replaced his impression with his extraordinary image,

which captured what he looks like now: a healthy young man who looks like other young men, who has friends and who has not once been rejected since his trauma, who has supported his clients to reach their dreams of top health. It includes his client, who bench-pressed more than 200kg, with his arm around him, and his son, who beams with pride for him.

Kenny put up recent photos of himself, including the one with his elated client, on his bathroom mirror. When he inserted his prosthetic eye in the morning and was reminded of what he looked like in hospital, he replaced the terrifying images with his updated image, capturing what he really looks like and capturing the meaning of his extraordinary belief.

5. Creating an Extraordinary Vision

Few people hold a vision for their life that extends beyond the current week. They may toy with notions of retiring one day or of completing a course or of having children. But picturing how they will shape different domains of their life to capture an extraordinarily fulfilling future is something most people don't think about unless they suffer a trauma.

Trauma forces people to re-evaluate and recreate their life. This book is about creating an extraordinary life without suffering trauma as a catalyst. Something I do with all my patients who suffer trauma and PTSD is to create a detailed picture of how they want their life to look in all domains: relationships, housing, job, finances, creativity, health, holidays and friends. We begin thinking about how to reclaim or rebuild their life in our first session. As therapy progresses, we create a ten-year vision and a five-year plan. Kenny was no exception. His vision for his life was certainly different having lost much of his eyesight and as we worked together, he became clearer about what was possible and what his bigger vision for his life would look like.

The first step in creating a vision for your life is to choose words to describe how you'd like your life to look in ten years. Much like how people describe their best version of themselves in the first paragraph of their CV, choose words to describe your best possible life. We choose ten years because it is long enough to capture major milestones, such as buying a house, having kids or retiring, that benefit from planning. Some people know they want to have kids, for example, but are unclear how they want their family situation to look or what steps would need to happen in the short term to ensure they reach their goals. Creating a longer-term vision helps to crystallise short-term steps and importantly, offers clarity about how to shape milestones to fit your desires.

Begin by making a note of how old you'll be ten years from now. Then choose words to describe how you'd like your life to feel at that age. For example, you may be forty-nine years old in ten years and choose words such as fulfilling, peaceful, content, healthy and fun. Or, you may be fifty-nine years old in ten years and choose words such as joyful, successful, busy, manageable, rewarding. Once you've got your descriptors, choose the one word that captures how you'd most often like your life to feel in the future. We carefully consider each domain, describing what each would look like if your life captured an extraordinary picture of the feeling you've chosen.How old will you be in ten years? Make a note in your journal and choose the words to describe your best possible life in ten years.

Kenny wrote: *In 10 years, I'll be 39. I want my life to consistently feel exciting, rewarding, successful and fulfilling.*

Then choose the one word that captures how you most often want your life to feel in ten years.

Kenny wrote: *In 10 years, I most often want my life to feel **fulfilling**.*

As you answer the questions below, substitute the example descriptor with the word you've chosen. Insert the word *extraordinarily* before it. For example, if the one word that captures how you want your life to feel in ten years' time is joyful, you would insert *extraordinarily* before *joyful* so you would be answering the questions in relation to creating an *extraordinarily joyful* life.

Most people find it tough to picture extraordinary possibilities when they are rooted in routine. It can be tough to think of developing a ground-breaking business when you're entrenched in a 9-to-5 job that brings a bit of satisfaction. Or to think of an extraordinary way of life when you are faced with never-ending responsibilities at home. The first step in thinking big is to discover what extraordinary means for you and then what would be extraordinary for you.

What is my big vision?

Leading an extraordinary life for one person may be starting a charity to help disadvantaged children. For another person, being extraordinary may be applying their best efforts to a monotonous job to give their children a top education or pursuing a passion in teaching despite feeling crippling self-doubt. For someone else, being extraordinary may be overcoming trauma and helping other people to flourish. We tend to see people as extraordinary when they achieve success despite traumatic circumstances or despite an ordinary past linked to little opportunity. For some people, being extraordinary taps enormous compassion for others, helping others to thrive.

Whatever your definition of extraordinary, being extraordinary requires the capacity to think bigger than one's perceived limitations, as well as the grit or determination to keep going when the going gets tough, the capacity to update painful memories to strengthen self-esteem and drive, the capacity to focus, to choose happiness rather than despair, the capacity to create a vision and stick to it and the capacity to draw on behaviours that support health and success. Each chapter of this book covers these factors. What we're doing here is creating your extraordinary vision.

Knowing what extraordinary means for you will support you as you answer the questions below. Hold your meaning of extraordinary in mind – we'll come back to it once we've created your biggest and best ten-year vision.

Knock your socks off

One of the ways I help clients to kick-start a frame of mind that could create compelling possibilities for their future is first to ask them to make a list of moments that knocked their socks off – moments when they remember feeling full of energy and buzzing with excitement.

When were you brimming with energy? When were you last buzzing with excitement?

People tend to buzz with greater energy when they are being spontaneous, creative, exercising vigorously, achieving something they didn't think possible or connecting with others. Kenny felt full of energy when he was helping clients solve their fitness challenges, which connected him to other people and tapped his creativity. Another one of my clients buzzed with excitement when she was designed new websites or when she was pushing herself in exercise with like-minded people. Whilst it may not be possible to exercise as a career, we can bring some of the achievement and excitement that comes from finishing a challenging workout into our everyday life by setting challenges, such as replying to ten emails in ten minutes or writing two reports in one hour, or making three calls to clients in fifteen minutes. It is possible to bring spontaneity into routine. But the point of the following exercise is to achieve some clarity on thinking big about what an extraordinary life could look like for you.

Let's start looking at each domain below.

As you answer the questions linked to each domain, substitute the example descriptor with the word you've chosen and noted above. Remember to insert *extraordinarily* before it.

Housing

What would your housing look like if you were leading an extraordinarily joyful life in ten years? (Remember to substitute *joyful* with the word you've chosen above). Who would you be living with? Where would you be living? The city or the countryside? Would you have pets or no pets? Children or no children? Elderly parents living with you, managing on their own or in care? Would you own your home or rent your home? **Then ask, how could your housing support you to feel full of energy?**

> Kenny wrote: *If I was leading an extraordinarily fulfilling life in ten years, I would own a flat in London with two bedrooms, one for my son and one for me. I would live in London most of the year except in winter when I would live in Ghana. My flat would need to have fun rooms for my son with sci-fi themes and quirky furniture, and a clear office space with a decent view for me to feel full of energy.*

Job

If you were leading an extraordinarily joyful life in ten years, what would your job look like? Would you be self-employed? Running your own business? Working for an organisation? A bit of both? Would you work part time or full time? Would you lead a team or be part of a team? How long would your commute be? Would you work flexible hours or would you work 9 to 5? Would you work weekends? **Then ask, what would you be responsible for in your work that would make you excited to start the day?**

Kenny wrote: *In ten years' time, I will be self-employed as a personal trainer, responsible for helping people to achieve physical strength after injury. This will excite me to start the day. I will also help disadvantaged pupils have an opportunity for education in Ghana. I will build an eco-friendly student hostel so students on low income will have a place to live while studying at the University of Ghana. I'll also be running my own business, supplying English skincare companies with top-quality shea butter.*

Relationship

Would you be in a relationship? Would you be living with your partner? Married or unmarried? Single and dating? Happily single and not dating? Would you be with the partner you have now or a new partner? Would you and your partner eat meals together on the weekend, during the week or both? **If you were leading an extraordinarily joyful life in ten years' time, how would your partner or friends describe you?**

Kenny wrote: *I won't be in a relationship, but I'll be dating. I'll be internet-dating and open to developing a relationship with a woman who loves kids, who is kind, funny and fun to be with, independent and happy to be apart a couple of months in a year. My friends will describe me as hard-working, reliable, interesting and kind.*

Finances

If you were leading an extraordinarily joyful life in ten years' time, what would your finances look like? Would you have saved a deposit for a house? Paid off your mortgage? Would you be debt-free? Would you own property? A car? Would you have investments? A pension? **How would your finances support you to feel excited about your life?**

> Kenny wrote: *I'll have saved for a deposit for a flat in London and will have secured a mortgage. I'll have started a savings account for my son's university fees. My finances will allow me to live in Ghana a few months a year without income, dedicating time to building sustainable student housing there. This will support me to feel excited about my life.*

Creativity

How would you spend your free time? What creative pursuits will you pursue, such as visiting museums or art galleries, or gardening, painting, walking or hiking? Creative pursuits are activities that absorb and connect you with a sense of stillness. What are these activities for you?

> Kenny wrote: *In my free time, I'll read about the basics to build sustainable housing in hot climates. I'll learn to make roof tiles. I'll ramble in nature when possible. I'll help my son learn to kickbox. I'll also read novels, sci-fi and I'll make movies from videos I take of my son.*

Health

If you were leading an extraordinarily joyful life in ten years' time, what would you be doing to support your health? Do you see yourself cooking more meals from scratch, eating out less often, eating less often? Exercising? Taking more time off work? Going to bed earlier and sleeping for longer? What will you comfortably be doing to support extraordinary health in ten years' time? Will you check your cholesterol regularly, your heart? Will you regularly step outdoors for fresh air and a break from routine?

> Kenny wrote: *I'll cook from scratch and make Ghanaian recipes. I'll continue to exercise daily. I'll keep up to date with advances in health and supplements. I will definitely keep taking my supplements. I'll spend a lot of time outdoors, especially when I'm working in Ghana.*

Holidays

Will you take holidays? Locally or further afield? If you were leading an extraordinarily joyful life, how many holidays would you take a year? Would you link them to work trips or as stand-alone trips? With family? With friends? With an partner? On your own? **How will your holidays support you to feel excited and buzzing with energy?**

> Kenny wrote: *Taking my son on holiday to Ghana will be exciting. I'd like to have two holidays a year, one around Christmas with my son, and a couple of breaks in Ghana when I'm working there. Exploring Ghana with my son is exciting and uplifting.*

Friends

How often would you see your friends? Would your friends visit you regularly or would you be more likely to plan outings? Would you celebrate birthdays together? Would you host regular parties or go to other people's parties? **What will you do with friends to support you to feel joyful, excited and full of energy?**

> Kenny wrote: *If I was leading an extraordinarily fulfilling life in ten years' time, I would see friends on weekends. We'd meet up for a drink or grab a meal together. About once a month, I'd meet with some friends to run the distance of half a marathon. Achieving challenges with friends would be fulfilling and I'd feel a lot of energy afterwards.*

Now that you've stretched your vision to see possibilities for all areas of your life, and you've thought through what goes into an extraordinary life, you're ready to design your dream work day and dream day off.

Your dream work day

What would your dream work day look like in ten years? What time do you get up? Are you alone or with a partner? Do you wake up with children around you? What is the first thing you do? How does your day unfold? Do you commute to an office? Or work at home? Go for a brisk walk? Describe a typical work day and a typical day off. **Underline what you are doing during the day that you're excited about, that makes you buzz with energy.**

> *Kenny – My dream work day – Extraordinarily Fulfilling*
>
> I wake up at 6, make a smoothie, take my supplements <u>and walk through the park</u> [**creativity**]. I warm up at the gym and <u>do my strength training</u> [**health**], then shower. I eat my favourite egg breakfast at the café next to the gym, then <u>plan my clients' training sessions for the day</u> [**job**]. I meet my first client at 9 a.m., <u>we review his goals and I push him hard</u> [**job**]. I have clients until 2, I walk home and make lunch and Jay's favourite snacks. I pick him up from school and take him to football practice. <u>I</u>

cheer his team on, give him some pointers [**creativity**] in breaks then we head home. I make dinner, we work on his maths home-work and I put him to bed. For the next hour or two, I check the progress of my Ghanaian hostel and the progress of setting up a bursary fund for pupils who need extra help [**job**].

Notice Kenny included one favourite activity during his work day. Kenny enjoys his egg breakfast at the café next to the gym. Research shows just how important to our well-being it is to include one enjoyable activity, however small, in our day's plan and how important it is to plan. You'll read throughout this book the science behind planning ahead, much of which has come out of my lab. People who learn to plan each day and to include an enjoyable activity in their plan show remarkable improvements in their well-being compared to people who do not plan ahead.

Kenny – My dream day off – Extraordinarily Fulfilling

I wake up at 7, I'm in Ghana, from my bed I have a view of the hostel I've been helping to build for the University of Ghana. My son pads into my room, we cuddle [**holiday**]. I get up and make us pancakes. He runs outside to play with other kids. I walk to the site and help with the roof for a few hours [**creativity & health**]. I grab lunch with a couple of mates on the site, my son and a couple of other kids join us then they run off to play. I carry on with the roof with the guys after lunch and go back to Jermayne's house for a BBQ dinner [**friends**]. We're there late, catching up with friends [**friends**], the kids playing. Jay and I head home around 11. I carry him, pop him into bed, shower and slip into sleep myself.

Notice Kenny includes enjoyable activities in his dream day off, some of which include connecting with other people. If possible, include an opportunity to connect with other people – your partner, children, friends, family or neighbours on your day off. This could be in person or on the telephone or through messages. Social connection helps to ward off blue feelings and keeps us upbeat.

Revisiting my extraordinary

As you read through your dream days, ask yourself if the vision you've created fits with your idea of extraordinary. Does your vision suggest that you've pictured a future inspired by possibility rather than doubt? How does your vision match your idea of extraordinary? If you need to edit your vision so it matches your concept of extraordinary, take a moment to do this now. Then move on to the next steps.

6. Your Step-by-Step Guide to Implementing Your Extraordinary Vision

Distilling outcomes into steps

Reread your dream days and look at what you've underlined that links to feeling excited. Which domains do they fall in?

The activities that excite and inspire Kenny on a work day tap his creativity, health and work domains. The activities that energise him on his day off fall into his holiday, creativity, friends and health domains.

The domains you've highlighted that link to feeling excited and buzzing with energy are the ones to prioritise in a five-year plan. Make a note of steps you'll need to take in each of these domains within a five-year time frame. What will you need to achieve in five years to ensure you're on track for an extraordinary ten years? Who and what resources will help you with your steps?

For Kenny to achieve his extraordinary ten-year vision filled with more rather than fewer days buzzing with energy and excitement, he must prioritise the domains linked to high energy in his dream days. There are four for Kenny: creativity, health, work and holiday domains.

Notice that some domains are achievable within a year. They are the areas that Kenny has already made great progress with. Some domains will need the full five years to come to fruition to lay the foundation for an extraordinary ten-year vision. Let's have a look at Kenny's five-year plan.

Kenny's Five-Year Plan

Health – Resources & Steps

-Look online for Ghanaian recipes.

-Check which shops might sell the ingredients.

-Try a Ghanaian recipe every Thursday night.

-Walk through the park to the gym tomorrow. Try this three times this week.

Achieve this in *[x] 1 year [ ] 2 years [ ] 3 years [ ] 4 years [ ] 5 years.*

Creativity – Resources & Steps

-Look online at sustainable housing sites.

-Order some books on Amazon.

-Speak to Matt who has built a sustainable office in his garden.

-Speak to locals in Ghana: which buildings are already sustainable? Who built them?

-*Read about roofing with sustainable tiles.*

-*Practise roofing on a makeshift roof, get good at it.*

-*Transfer my skills to a real roof.*

Achieve this in *[ ] 1 year [ ] 2 years [x] 3 years [ ] 4 years [ ] 5 years.*

Holiday – Resources & Steps

-*Chat with my ex-girlfriend about taking Jay on holiday to Ghana for a month. Start the chat by email, suggest we meet to discuss.*

-*Speak to my friend, Amy, who's a communication coach. Pick up some pointers about how to phrase my email to my ex-girlfriend.*

-*Negotiate Christmas dates with my ex-girlfriend. Usually goes smoothly, can do this next month.*

-*Speak to my friends about fun, different kids' stuff I could do at Christmas.*

-*Look online for different Christmas ideas.*

Achieve this in *[x] 1 year [ ] 2 years [ ] 3 years [ ] 4 years [ ] 5 years.*

Job – Resources & Steps

ECO-FRIENDLY STUDENT HOSTEL

- *Speak to the university in Ghana. Can they offer any support for the building project?*

-*The land I've bought is close to the university. Make arrangements for planning permission, seek the support of the university.*

-*Chat to locals and local companies. Determine who would be good to have on the project.*

-Hire a project manager I trust and can communicate with from the UK.

-Once the hostel is built, plan to furnish and decorate the interior.

SHEA BUTTER COMPANY

-Make a business plan for my shea butter company. I'll need to talk to friends who have experience with importing products to the UK.

-Research online courses on starting your own business.

-I can feasibly dedicate one hour a week starting Wednesday to work on my new business, gathering information, thinking through websites, making contacts with shea butter farmers in Ghana, learning about import restrictions in the UK, contacting skincare companies and learning about trade shows.

Achieve this in *[ ] 1 year [ ] 2 years [ ] 3 years [ ] 4 years [x] 5 years.*

The domain for Kenny that requires the longest long-term planning is his work domain. This may also be the case for you. To achieve a dream work day, which inspires, motivates and excites you, typically requires lots of long-term planning. Since it is usually our work that fills most of our time, it is often this area that needs the most tweaking to drive extraordinary success and joy.

Work backwards

The next step is to look at the domains you've noted you'd like to achieve within one year and work backwards. Take a sheet of paper or open a new blank document, write the twelve months of the year, and for each one, bullet-point what you need to achieve month-by-month to ensure you're on track to achieve the goal within the year. Then look at the domains that have goals you'd like to achieve within two to five years and note which steps need prep within the year and assign the prep to the months you've noted. Then work backwards again. Write Week 1, 2, 3, 4 for the current month only and bullet-point what you need to achieve week-by-week to ensure you're on track for that month. Open your calendar, look at the coming week and schedule the tasks you need to achieve that week. At the end of the week, assess your progress and adjust your plan for the coming week, scheduling tasks you didn't quite finish and rescheduling tasks that are no longer possible in the short term given work and family commitments. At the end of the month, assess your progress and reassess the bullet points for the next month, assigning them to the weeks of the month.

Taking a monthly and weekly view whilst holding your big vision in mind helps you to manage time and overcome the tendency to schedule what you're keen to wrap up rather than what is feasible to achieve. Planning and replanning will keep you on track whilst keeping you connected to your bigger vision.

7. How to Stick to Your Plan

The real key to sticking to your plan is to get started. Of course, making your plan feasible, visible and achievable is absolutely necessary. But starting then finishing a step, however small, towards your bigger vision gives a sense of achievement and a burst of dopamine, and strengthens your desire to take more steps, which means you'll be more likely to make your big vision your reality. Spot and take small steps towards your big vision most days of the week. This will keep it at the forefront of your mind, give you bursts of dopamine to keep you going with more steps, and give you tangible progress bringing you closer to greater success. Of course, there are top tips to help. The ones outlined here are tried and tested, many of which Kenny used to create his thriving businesses.

Get started

Easier said than done, right? How do you get started on creating an extraordinary life? If you've answered the questions to spot your bigger vision and distilled outcomes into steps as above, then look at the plan you've created and your schedule for the coming week. Ask yourself: what can I do this week towards my bigger vision? The aim is to incorporate one small step every day – to make it a part of your life so building your extraordinary future is not something that you set aside for when you have a spare few hours, but something you're weaving into your every day. In my experience with clients, setting the expectation to do something every day means you'll likely achieve it three times a week – which is a lot more than not at all. Chapter V, Extraordinary Behaviours, has more tips on getting started if you are struggling to begin new behaviours that will support success with your bigger vision.

Focus on feasibility

Are the steps you're planning to take in the short term feasible given the pressures on your time? If it's not feasible or if it feels draining to chat to friends in the coming week who have key contacts you may need to reach out to, plan to do this during half-term or at the weekend, when you may have a few extra minutes. Creating a plan with a feasible time frame for achieving your steps increases your likelihood of actually reaching them. Every time you achieve a step you give yourself a win, a tiny burst of dopamine, which is a deserving pat on the back. The burst of dopamine reinforces the link between taking a step and feeling good. This is helpful – it means that you'll feel good achieving steps, and this will motivate you to keep going. The other thing that happens when you achieve steps is that you strengthen your extraordinary belief – yes, you really can do it – which means you'll be stronger in facing any setbacks on your path.

Passion is in the picture

This chapter has been all about images. Most images are visual. The message here . . . picture your final destination, of you living your dream days. Create this picture in your mind's eye and call it to mind often. Don't let today's routines bury your best vision for your life. Find an actual photo that captures the essence of what you're working to achieve and make it your screensaver on your phone, laptop or tablet or all three. Print it out and frame it. Make sure you see it. Kenny framed the photo of his client achieving the 200kg bench press. The more visible your vision, the more likely you'll see it, feel a pull to create it, and take steps towards bringing it to fruition. In moments of self-doubt, look at the picture you've created (just as Kenny did – he put it in front of his bathroom mirror so it was the first thing he saw every morning) – or call it to mind and see it vividly in your mind's eye just as elite athletes call to mind pictures of their ultimate success.

Accountability with a deadline

Who or what is going to increase your level of accountability? Who will step up and nudge you when you're tempted by a third night of Netflix? The more you can create a level of accountability with deadlines, the more likely you'll follow through on achieving the steps you've set for yourself. Draw on your friends for support or hire a coach in the short term to help you to meet your steps. Talk to your kids about your plan so you're accountable to them too. Join the Be Extraordinary community on www.beextraordinary book.com where you can buddy up with a group of project leaders, schedule group chats, post your progress and set your goals for the next month. Here you can read people's success stories, their progress with projects, and post encouraging comments on next steps. Other people will also have the opportunity to post reassuring comments on your next steps. People love hearing about progress with projects, and reading people's encouraging comments will motivate you to keep going.

Make it visible

Write your steps in your calendar so every time you look at your schedule, you see the step you need to achieve that day. If you get through a day without finishing up the step you had planned, break it into two smaller steps and redo your plan for the next day, including one of the smaller steps, if possible. If your next day is chock-a-block, schedule a small step when you know you can feasibly manage it. People who transition from ordinary to extraordinary continually redo their plans until they're quite skilled at knowing what is feasible given their commitments and can successfully schedule tasks they know they'll be able to complete.

Give yourself breaks

Make sure you link rewards to achieving milestones as well as monotonous tasks. If you need to fire off twenty-two emails to arrange three appointments, make sure you reward yourself with two minutes of downtime surfing the net or enjoying a piece of cake or your favourite coffee. Linking rewards to monotonous tasks makes them manageable and lays the foundation for the bigger, more important tasks. There are more details on how to use breaks to support productivity in the chapter on Focus.

8. How to Keep Going When the Going Gets Tough

It's inevitable as you work towards your bigger vision (which, let's face it, covers a good few years) that you'll hit a setback on the path, a moment where something doesn't go as planned – a business plan is rejected by the bank, a business partner walks out or an investor gives you cutting feedback on your pitch. Or perhaps it's a personal setback – your wife files for divorce, a close family member dies or the company you're working for goes bust. What then? These are tough events and, of course, it's natural for self-doubt to creep in or for strong emotions to take over.

What will help you through these tough times is to call to mind your extraordinary belief wrapped with an image. It will help you to navigate to choices that are compassionate and smart whilst also bringing you back to the track of extraordinary when you're ready. In these times, ask yourself: what would someone who is 100 per cent [insert your extraordinary belief] do in this situation? For example, what would someone who is 100 per cent innovative, creative, hard-working, proactive and strong do in this situation? What would [insert the people who most want you to succeed] suggest you do in this situation? Then picture your empowering image, the image encapsulating your extraordinary belief, of you succeeding with the people who would most relish your success spurring you on. Seeing the picture of you succeeding in your mind's eye will strengthen your confidence. Picturing the kind faces of the people who most want you to succeed will help you to tap compassion, which will lower stress hormones leading to more effective problem-solving.

How Can You Take This Forward?

Our impressions and images of ourselves influence our choices, behaviours and even how people see us. They give clues about niggling self-doubts, which can hold us back and make it tougher to plan for success. It is these negative images and niggling self-doubts that have to go because they determine whether or not we'll start and keep to the path to extraordinary.

People who transition from ordinary to extraordinary take control of their images, they create winning images and call them to mind frequently. Creating an image to support extraordinary success means first digging deep to uncover the worst meaning of a limiting image, which may be linked to an earlier memory. Updating the worst meaning lays the foundation for building an extraordinary belief that will drive you to thrive.

Work through the steps in this chapter to learn how to spot limiting images or impressions and how to update their worst meanings. Reboot your beliefs for success with the steps outlined here and wrap your extraordinary belief with an image. Call it to mind often. Remember, focused imagery in your mind's eye is a lot like giving yourself a real experience. You can strengthen your neural circuitry for success with imagery. Once you've got your image in place, create your ten-year vision and five-year plan. The questions in this chapter will energise your bigger vision and drive your desire to get started and to keep going. Use a journal, give yourself a couple of hours and the attention this process deserves to set a solid foundation for transitioning from ordinary to extraordinary.

In a Nutshell

Elite athletes top up their training with images of success.

Images are pictures we create in our mind's eye. They also include impressions, our sense of ourselves and our capacity for success.

Everyone has an image or impression of themselves. But we're often unaware of them.

Images affect how we feel and behave, and in some cases how people perceive us.

Negative images and impressions are limiting. They're linked to highly charged thoughts and extreme beliefs. They keep us stuck in a rut.

The worst meaning of your images operates like a prejudice against yourself. It will hold a sense of inadequacy.

People who transition from ordinary to extraordinary create motivating images that capture empowering beliefs. They frequently call their images to mind.

Updating a limiting meaning linked to a limiting image requires you to
o Re-evaluate it
o Look at facts

o Reorientate your focus. Notice achievements

Creating an extraordinary image for success requires you to

o Reboot your beliefs – what is the best meaning of your achievements?
o Wrap your extraordinary belief with an empowering image

Images that motivate extraordinary behaviour include details of succeeding. They also include the person or people we most aspire to make proud.

Creating a ten-year vision and a five-year plan will guide you to create an extraordinarily fulfilling future.

Top Tips for Sticking to your Five-year Plan
o Get started
o Make it feasible
o Make it visible
o Increase your accountability
o Picture success
o Approach setbacks through the lens of your extraordinary belief
o Give yourself breaks

II.

Fluid Memory

If you've ever suffered a setback like blanking in an interview before breaking the silence with waffle that buries you or, even worse, suffered a trauma like the sudden death of a loved one, you'll know first hand that the memories you most want to forget are the ones you'll most remember.

Those snippets from events long gone can disrupt your day and make you feel exactly as you did when you lived through the event you wished you'd never had. It's natural to push messy memories out of mind when they pop up, but this only keeps their messiness around for longer, making them more likely to intrude again and again.

People who transition from ordinary to extraordinary clean up their memories. They scoop up their difficult times, dust off the dirt and change their painful meanings. No matter what they live through, they create a meaningful relationship to their past that ensures an extraordinary future. They recreate their memories, rewrite the bad times, not by changing the facts of what happened, but by changing the meaning of their challenging times.

Rewriting our memories is called *updating*, where we update the worst meaning of the memory. It's a process that keeps our memories fluid and is in keeping with what the brain naturally does when we remember an event: rewrite it.

To lead an extraordinary future, we must master our memories. This means creating fluid memories, so we're not interrupted throughout the day by intrusive memories. And it means learning to unhook the present from past events that fuel self-doubt.

In this chapter, we'll look at hot-off-the-press science findings to discover how the brain makes then recreates memories. We'll discover why it's important to update our troublesome memories, and how to do it. We'll learn from Joshua, a young American soldier who was shot on a humanitarian aid mission, survived against the odds, then successfully appealed US Congress for funds to support soldiers with their emotional recovery from combat. We'll transform our everyday stressors and difficult memories, so they motivate rather than defeat us.

People who transition from ordinary to extraordinary update their memories, whether they're tough trauma memories or everyday annoyances. Transitioning from ordinary to extraordinary taps a capacity to make memories rich and fluid rather than disorganised and stuck.

Joshua's Story

Joshua, a twenty-four-year-old American soldier, was shot in Iraq on a humanitarian aid mission for children. During the sniper attack, a 50-calibre bullet shot through and killed his staff sergeant, Marlin Harpur, and landed in Joshua's right leg. Joshua died . . . for fifteen minutes. The brigade surgeon shocked his heart and injected adrenalin into his body every three minutes. He was about to give up when a faint pulse returned. He knew Joshua would be brain-damaged. He had been medically dead for more than six minutes. But the miracle is that he is not. Joshua survived his attack with a severely wounded leg and the death of a close comrade. He made it his mission to speak to CNN, Fox TV, ABC and the *New*

York Times in order to publicise his case for appealing the US Congress to increase funds for US troops to support their emotional recovery from combat. He is now a major contributor to the Wounded Warriors Project. Joshua updated his memory of himself, with effort, from being a fit soldier on duty, to being killed and weakened, and finally, to being a soldier who survived with a wealth of knowledge to help other soldiers deal with the emotional stress of combat.

1. What Is Memory?

In its simplest terms, memory is storage of information. I like to think of memory as running along a continuum that looks like a cone, capturing changes in storage from milliseconds to decades. So, at one end we have fleeting memories, stored for milliseconds, the stream of sensory information our brains are continually processing – what we see, hear, taste, touch and feel in any moment. A little further along the continuum sits working memory or short-term memory, which offers storage capacity from a few seconds to a few minutes. At the far end rests long-term memory, which can hold information for a lifetime.

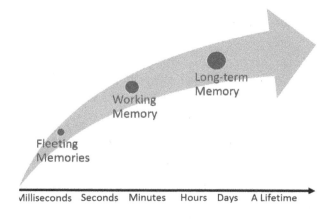

When we talk of memory, what we're really referring to is a process of input, storage and retrieval. We normally think of this process in relation to memories that last longer than a few minutes, our long-term memories for facts called *semantic memory*, or memories for events, called *episodic memories*.

Our memories shape who we are. They influence our decisions and plans, helping us to problem-solve, prepare and imagine our future. It was once thought that when the brain made a long-term memory, what it was really doing was compiling a permanent file and that the process of remembering required the brain to search through the folds of the cortex and dig out the file where it would be returned unchanged after use ... because it was, after all, a permanent record.

But early in the twenty-first century, Karim Nader and Joseph LeDoux blew away the idea of the permanence of memory with experiments that showed the opposite – the malleability of memory. They trained rats to learn that a box was dangerous by shocking their paws when they were in the box. The next time the rats were put back in the box, they froze in fear.

Since neurons synthesise proteins to make a memory, if the memory was a permanent trace, then giving drugs to block protein synthesis after a few days should make no difference to the rats' ability to remember the box as dangerous. Reminding the rats of how dangerous the box is before giving the drug also should make no difference to their ability to remember their fear since, according to traditional theory, the memory was already a permanent trace.

Memories are malleable, changeable, flexible.

So, after a few days, the researchers gave drugs to block protein synthesis. They drugged the rats before reminding them of the box or after a brief reminder of the box. If they drugged the rats before reminding them of the box, this made no difference to their ability to remember what they had learned: the box was dangerous, and they froze in fear. But if the rats had a brief reminder of the box before the drug was given, the memory of the dangerousness of the box seemed to be erased. Reactivating the memory had put it up for grabs and to be remembered, it had to go through the brain's memory-making process again – to be reconsolidated. But it couldn't because protein synthesis had been blocked.

This was a ground-breaking discovery. But was it reliable? Perhaps the original memory trace hadn't been well consolidated. Perhaps the researchers had tested recall too soon after teaching the rats to associate fear with the box.

So, Nader and LeDoux repeated the experiment. Again, they taught rats to fear the box by shocking their paws when they were in there. Then, they waited forty-five days before repeating the rest of the experiment. They waited this length of time since, as the theory goes, the brain needs a month to make a long-term memory. Their idea was that the dangerousness of the box would definitely be a long-term memory by forty-five days. They injected the rats with drugs to block protein synthesis. The rats who had no reminder of the box before their injection retained their fear memory of the box. The rats who were reminded of the box before the drug lost their memory for what had happened and showed no fear or freeze response when they were put back in there.

Reactivating the memory of the fearful box then stopping the brain from re-forming the memory caused the rats to forget their trauma. This suggests that long-term memories need to be reconsolidated when recalled or they'll be wiped out.

So there we have it. Memory is malleable. Or rather, rat memories are malleable. What we'll see shortly is that our memories are too.

Our memories are pliable like putty

Quite a few things (it seems like almost anything) can change what we recall – how a question is phrased, what we're feeling, how much we've slept, how we see ourselves and whether we're better able to remember facts or stories.

Even replacing a dry word for a juicier one changes what people remember. Memory expert Elizabeth Loftus is responsible for this memory finding. She showed students short clips of car crashes then invited them to describe what they'd seen. Afterwards, she asked a question about the speed of the cars, varying the word she chose to describe the point of impact. Some students were asked, 'How fast were the cars going when they *smashed* into each other?' She asked other students the same question, but instead of 'smashed' she used the word 'collided' 'bumped' 'hit' or 'contacted'.

> Replacing a dry word for a juicy one changes what people remember.

What happened? The juicier words created speedier cars in people's memories. Using the word 'smashed' led to memories with the highest estimates of speed (40.8 mph) followed by 'collided' (39.3 mph) and 'bumped' (38.1 mph), all much higher than the word 'contacted' (31.8 mph). Hence Loftus concluded that language can alter recall.

But sceptics were hot on her heels to suggest that the memory of the car crash was intact and what had changed was how students described it rather than students changing their memory to fit the words they heard.

Back to the lab. In the follow-up experiment, Loftus showed students another car crash. Fifty of them were asked how fast the cars were going when they 'hit' each other, another fifty were asked how fast the cars were going when they 'smashed' each other and another fifty weren't asked anything.

One week later, the students were asked if they saw broken glass. Students were more likely to remember seeing broken glass if, in the week before, they had been asked to estimate the speed of the cars when they 'smashed' each other.

> The language you use to describe your memories can help or hinder you.

But there was no broken glass! The findings have been hugely important for guiding interviews of eyewitnesses to crime. The experiment showed that something seemingly harmless, like changing one word in a question, can change what people remember, leading to fair or, as in the case of false convictions, unfair consequences.

What this means is that the language you use to describe your memories can help or hinder you. For example, when you remember a job interview where you performed less than your best, choose words to describe the experience that will support future success, rather than language likely to keep you spinning the wheel of mediocrity.

Repeatedly recalling, and hence rewriting the memory, with colourful yet extreme words could hinder your beliefs about yourself, ultimately making it harder to choose strategies for success. 'I royally stuffed up and waffled my way through the tough questions' is likely to fuel beliefs linked to inadequacy or incompetence. When we believe we're unworthy, inadequate or incompetent, it's much harder to dust ourselves off and write a winning job application.

Why make the process of success more challenging right at the outset, when you could start from a supportive base? Simply changing a few words will tip you towards future success. A job interview that did not go well could become 'The questions were hard, and I did my best. Ultimately it was a useful experience to help prep me for future interviews.'

What does this mean for troublesome memories?

It's possible to change memories. And it's necessary. If we think about it, memory has to be malleable for us to lead our lives. The malleability of memory allows us to integrate new learning with old learning, to correct mistakes in our life stories and to imagine the future.

> It's possible to change memories ... for better or for worse.

Rewriting memories is a process we do many times a day as we recall the past. People who transition from ordinary to extraordinary rewrite their memories to nourish beliefs and behaviours that will motivate future success.

Patients who recover from PTSD also update their memories. Their memories of trauma at the end of therapy are more rich and fluid, flowing between the past and the present, than when they started therapy. When they remember their trauma, they weave information from the present that updates their worst moment in the past. For example, if a patient survived a head-on collision and their worst fear at the time was that they would die, meaning they would never again see their children, their updated memory at the end of therapy would be something like: 'I saw the lorry coming towards me and I thought, That's it, I'll die, I'll never see my kids. **Now I know I survived, I see my children every day, I walk with them to school.** The next thing I remember in my accident is hearing the sirens of the ambulance, a man asking me a lot of questions and feeling a strong urge to sleep. The paramedics had arrived, and I knew I was going to be helped.' The updated memory updates the worst meaning with information from the present.

Troublesome memories that have absorbed new information are spongy and much less likely to become springy – that is, intrusive. The earlier you can link new information to a troublesome memory, the less likely it will bother you in the long run.

Does it work?

To discover the effects of updating a troublesome memory early on, my students and I first simulated trauma in over 100 people. Everyone watched films of people dying in car crashes. Then we gave one group information about what actually happened. Even though the outcome was awful, we told them the facts. The facts were that the people in the films did not survive, they died. Then we added a crucial piece of new information . . . their suffering is over. We gave no extra information to the other group.

Both groups watched the films again. In the weeks that followed, the group with new information were free from PTSD symptoms even though they had watched gruelling scenes of people dying and knew they were dying. Their

> The aim is to make troublesome memories more spongy, so they are less springy.

memory had soaked up the new information like a sponge and perhaps, like a soggy sponge, their memory was less springy and never sprung to mind in the next week. They had protected themselves from getting PTSD simply by updating their memories.

Whereas for the folk who got no new information, who saw the same heart-wrenching scenes of people dying without the added information that they were no longer suffering, well, their memories were springy, bouncing in and out of mind in the following weeks.

What does this tell us about how to deal with unwanted memories – whether it's an embarrassing memory or a traumatic memory?

Weaving new and true information into a troublesome memory helps to update the worst meaning of the memory and keep it rolling forward rather than keeping it stuck at the very worst moment.

Even mice do it!

Even mice update their memories. By looking at which neurons light up in mice when they overcome a fearful association, Johannes Graff and his team were able to determine that neurons linked to new learning light up and connect to the neurons associated with the original fear memory. They concluded that the new learning weaves with the original memory to rewrite it rather than forming a new memory that suppresses the fearful one.

And the extraordinary

People who transition from ordinary to extraordinary update their worst moments. They don't change the facts of the past. If an accident happened, it happened. If someone died, they died. If they weren't hired after a job interview, they weren't hired. These are the facts. But what they update is the worst meaning. Weaving new and true information with the facts of what happened makes the memory fluid and takes away the sting.

2. Everyday Memories

Memories with an emotional thread of shame, guilt or anger are more likely to spring to mind when we don't want them to. Once popped up, they can disrupt our day, our focus, and make us feel rubbish, ultimately keeping us stuck in a rut.

The best way to smooth out tricky day-to-day memories is to take a moment to think about their worst meaning and update the worst meaning with facts. Then include the updated meaning in the memory. For example, my patient Carina blanked in a job interview then buried any chance for recovery with wasted minutes of waffle. She felt ashamed, thinking about what she'd say to her friends.

To get back on an extraordinary track, we first spotted what she believed the memory said about her as a person. I asked, 'What does not getting the job say about you as a person?' She believed it meant she was stupid and incompetent and would never succeed in her career. Carina spotted how such a belief was keeping her stuck in a rut and how she was using the memory as evidence to support her unhelpful belief.

We updated her belief about being stupid and incompetent. She had a lot of evidence she was clever and a problem-solver – she had achieved her degree while also providing the best possible care for her mum. She had also been hired in the summer by a local charity to write reports for their trustees. The problem was Carina was just not focusing on this evidence. Carina updated her unhelpful belief to something more accurate that would motivate success: 'I'm clever, a problem-solver and already have some success under my belt.' She trained her mind to look for evidence to fit her new belief rather than filter day-to-day events to support a stuck-in-a-rut belief. She also worked on the strategies in Chapter I to boost beliefs for extraordinary success.

Importantly, Carina re-examined the memory through the lens of her updated belief. If she fully believed she was clever and a problem-solver, how would she rewrite the memory of missing success in her job interview? Carina focused on the facts, the new and true information:

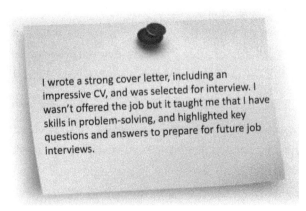

I wrote a strong cover letter, including an impressive CV, and was selected for interview. I wasn't offered the job but it taught me that I have skills in problem-solving, and highlighted key questions and answers to prepare for future job interviews.

When the memory popped to mind, Carina linked the new and true information to the memory and then carried on with her day, more confident to reapply for jobs than dwell on the past.

The everyday memory does not stop at the worst moment but includes information that updates the worst meaning.

UNSTICKING EVERYDAY MEMORIES

SPOT
- The answers to the questions
  - o What's so bad about it?
  - o What does it say about you as a person?

INVESTIGATE LIKE A DETECTIVE
- How accurate is the worst meaning?
- What evidence do you have today to weaken the worst meaning?
- What did you learn in the event that could help you in the future?

UPDATE YOUR BELIEF
- Update your belief with facts not feelings
  - o Carina didn't get hired after interview for a job she wanted and believed this meant she was stupid and incompetent. She updated her belief with facts linked to her achievements
- See the memory through the lens of the updated belief or your extraordinary belief then flatten that memory with facts

CONNECT THE PRESENT TO THE PAST
- When the memory pops to mind, fast forward to what you know now, facts that update the worst meaning
  - o Carina's memory never stopped at the worst moment
  - o It went on to include her new information

THEN TUNE TO THE TASK AT HAND
- Once you've polished up your memory, refocus on your task at hand

Arguments

What about the blazing row you had with your boyfriend last night? Or the one with your daughter when she asked if she could stay out late . . . again? It's tough to shake these grievances and as you're typing emails at work, memories of incredulous accusations come to mind, snatching your attention without solving the issues that caused you to clash. How do you deal with these types of everyday memories?

Well, there's one thing we know for sure. Your sparring partner is going to have a different memory of your argument. Why? Well, remember what we learned about memory? Almost anything can change what we remember – a juicy word, what we're feeling, how much we've slept, how we see ourselves and whether we're better able to remember facts or stories.

When your partner or daughter remembers the argument, their brain is building the memory around scaffolding that rests on how much sleep has been had, the words chosen to guide recall ('I had a blazing row with my mum' will lead to a different memory than 'my mum and I disagreed about what time I could stay out until'), and what kind of memory-maker the person is – better able to remember facts or vivid personal stories. Hopefully it will be the former. Someone better able to remember rich personal stories is more likely to have a mind that stamps pictures to memories. Imagine your daughter re-remembering you screaming rather than chatting (you don't scream) because her mind has painted a picture to fit her story. Doesn't bear thinking about.

Your memories are going to be, at worst, wildly different and, at best, annoying. So instead of dwelling on the incredulous things that were said, see the memory intrusion as a cue to disengage from it and take care of yourself, whether that's refocusing on what you are actually doing (typing those emails), getting up and out for a get-out-of-your head brisk walk or making a cuppa. Giving yourself a break helps you to tap compassion and from a compassionate place you can solve life's problems or your daughter's problems with a clearer head. Seriously. Compassion helps us to problem-solve better so it's far better to be kind to yourself than to torture your day chewing argument gum.

ARGUMENTS

REMEMBER THE SCIENCE
- You and your sparring partner will have wildly different memories of the same event
- Giving yourself a break helps you to tap compassion
- Compassion lowers stress hormones and makes us better problem-solvers . . . to solve the problems that started the rows

USE THE MEMORY INTRUSION TO YOUR ADVANTAGE . . . A CUE TO GIVE YOURSELF A BREAK
- Refocus on what you're actually doing, like all those emails
- Get up and out for a get-out-of-your-head brisk walk
- Make a cuppa

Why are some memories easily triggered?

The short answer is . . . because of how they've been encoded.

We can learn a lot about why some memories are triggered while others aren't by first discovering how the brain deals with a traumatic memory. During a trauma, adrenalin is coursing through the

63

body transforming your brain into a high-speed processor, able to encode information you normally wouldn't pay much attention to. The brain over-encodes sensory information – what you see, hear, taste, smell and feel – cementing these details as warning signs for danger. After trauma, when your brain spots a similar detail to the past event, alarm bells ring and you're flooded in fear with the memory racing back to mind. You'll feel like the trauma's about to happen again or something equally terrifying.

The brain's ability to over-encode information is all well and good when our event is a wild boar we're trying to escape as we run back to our Stone Age caves. But it's less clever when the trauma that hits us is a car or person. We can't avoid cars or people forever and the reality is that most people and cars are safe.

People who develop PTSD have brains that are really good at one kind of learning, associative learning, and less able to unlearn associations or to naturally break the link between trauma in the past and triggers in the present.

Similar processes also apply to other unpleasant events, like being bullied, humiliated or embarrassed. We give these events a lot of attention so that we can avoid similar situations in the future. We over-remember them and when matching triggers present themselves, the memories and associated feelings come flooding back.

It's the worst moments that typically intrude into our minds. They hold the gruelling meaning of the memory. So, when they come back to mind, you may feel all the difficult feelings linked to the worst meaning of that moment.

Joshua's worst moment was losing the feeling in his legs as he lay on the operating table, realising he was dying, that he would never see his mother or baby sister again. He believed they would suffer and that he was letting them down. When he was revived, physically recovered and back in the US, his trauma memory was easily triggered by appointments in hospitals, of which he had many, TV medical dramas and lying down. These triggers brought to mind his worst moment and he felt all over again the fear, loss and sadness he felt at the time.

Breaking the links to the past

Part of being extraordinary means living your life unencumbered by the past. We've all lived through events we wish had never happened, such as messing up an important talk, being overlooked for a job promotion, rejected by a romantic partner, bullied at school, or even worse, beaten or abused as a kid.

Unfair and tough events at any age can shape how we think about ourselves. Our minds are especially impressionable when we're young. We're more likely to see a harsh event as proof that, at our core, we're incompetent, unworthy, unlovable or stupid, rather than proof that the other people involved are inadequate, unkind and unwell. Such beliefs can hold us back rather than motivate and support our extraordinary success. Even if we do succeed, with these sorts of experiences under our belt, we may feel that our success is temporary and it's only a matter of time before the real incompetent, unworthy and stupid person at the core is discovered.

> Being extraordinary means breaking the links to events that fuel self-doubt.

As adults, we're responsible for taking care of our own needs. But this wasn't the case when we were kids. We may have had parents or other adults around us who were ill equipped to meet our needs. We were at the mercy of the choices they made, which may have put us in harm's way at some point during our child-hood. As adults, we rarely experience the same things we did as kids. Until we break the links with the past, though, we may feel like we're on the brink of rejection, criticism or some form of abuse, which can keep us acting meek and mild rather than confident and proactive.

How do I break the links to the past?

When there is rubbish you've lived through, **first recognise you got through.** This in itself is an accomplishment. Well done. You got through it. And you likely learned from it. At the very least, you learned you won't treat other people in the same way you were treated. **Second, flip it.** What this means is take a step back and ask yourself what the event says about the other people involved. Forget what you've been telling yourself it means about you. You may conclude that the event is bona fide proof that the other people involved are unkind, unskilled and in some ways incompetent. Third, **break the link** between the past event and the present by spotting all the ways now is different to then. Finally, recall your extraordinary belief you worked on in Chapter I, Vision, and **tune to day-to-day evidence that supports the new belief** not the limiting one.

What's Then vs Now?

Then vs Now is a trauma-treatment strategy first developed by my colleague Anke Ehlers at the University of Oxford as part of her highly effective treatment for PTSD. Then vs Now helps you to process the present without being haunted by the past. It's a strategy that focuses your attention on all the ways now is different to then.

Triggers to past unpleasant events tend to be scattered around our surroundings. But triggers can also be subtle and internal. They can be feelings or body sensations that match a similar feeling or body sensation to a past event. For example, if you were bullied in the past and felt panicked, when you have a similar feeling today, such as feeling panicked when your boss asks for progress on your report, you may feel as though you're about to be attacked verbally or physically.

> Then vs Now helps you to spot all the ways now is different to then, which unhooks the present from the past.

What's happened here is that the feeling of panic is similar in the past and in the present. In the past, the feeling of panic preceded being attacked. In the present the feeling of panic makes you feel like you're about to be attacked.

You have to help your brain to unhook the present from the past. The most immediate way to do this is to focus on how *now* is different to then. Focus on how your boss has never attacked you, but perhaps has mostly responded to you in a kind and friendly way. Spot that you are at work in an office and not in the playground at school. Spot that you are safe and spot the ways you are valued by the people you work with. Focusing on how now is different to then helps your brain to process the present without pressure from the past.

Often painful experiences are triggered without our recollection. This is not to say that we have lost our memory for them, it means that they can be triggered without us being aware that they've been triggered, a process psychologists have called 'affect without recollection'.

When you feel less than your best and infused with self-doubt, which seems to be out of proportion to the situation you're in, ask yourself when you first remember feeling this way. Is there some similarity, subtle and internal like a similar feeling, or a matching trigger in your surroundings that links to a past unpleasant event? If so, spot all the ways now is different to then.

Begin simply by noting where you are, what you see, who you are with and how all of these things are different to the past event. Importantly, spot that you are in control, and you choose how you lead your life and what you believe about yourself. Then remind yourself of your extraordinary belief and tune to evidence to support it.

Exceptional memories

Exceptional memories are memories for events, such as a car accident, injury or break-up, that have disrupted your life temporarily or, in some cases, permanently. Exceptional memories are troublesome when they grab your attention and make you feel anxious, as though you're reliving the event you wish you'd never had. Or, when you're seeing them as evidence for a stuck-in-a-rut belief.

How do you update troublesome memories?

The tools that update troublesome memories are the same ones that help to update trauma memories. They were first developed by my colleague Anke Ehlers and her team in Oxford to help people recover from PTSD.

To update troublesome memories, follow these five steps:

1. Spot the worst meaning

2. Update the meaning

3. Link the new meaning to the worst moment

4. Make it stick

5. Use *Then vs Now*

Spot the worst meaning

The first step is to spot which part of the memory is causing the sting, then find information to soothe it. This means we uncover the worst meaning of the memory then find information that makes the meaning of the memory less threatening. In short, we update the memory by updating the meaning.

This is usually pretty straightforward. If someone crashed their car and thought they were going to die at the time, the information that we link to the terrifying memory of the car crash is that they survived.

Then to help the memory nestle more smoothly with other memories, we go one step further to uncover the worst meaning of dying and other details which prove the person's worst fears didn't happen (if they didn't happen). Then we link all this information to the memory, and the troublesome memory becomes trouble-free.

But how do you discover the worst thing about dying? Is it really necessary?

Starting with the last question first, yes it's totally necessary to discover the worst meaning of people's worst moments. We can't change the facts of the past, but we can soften the blow to make the memory less troublesome. New and true information, which updates the worst meaning, makes troublesome memories more spongy and less springy.

And back to the first question . . . how do you discover the worst thing about dying?

I ask eyebrow-raising questions to get to the worst of the worst. 'What would be so bad about dying?' Or, 'What's the worst thing about dying for you?'

This kind of work can be awkward. Imagine sitting opposite a person who has just told you that a lorry lost control on the M4 and their car was totalled; emergency services cut them out of their crumpled vehicle before they were air-lifted to hospital and they confide that they thought that was it, their life was over, they were sure they would die. And you nod empathetically and then say . . . 'And what would be so bad if you did die?'

The answer, of course, is different for everyone. For some people, the worst thing about dying is realising they've traded opportunities for happiness with hours of monotony and now won't have the chance to pursue their real passion. For other people, it's about being robbed of all the future good times with their kids. For someone else, it's about the anguish their parents would feel with their loss.

In my twenty years of practice, I have yet to uncover the meaning of dying that is exactly the same for any two people.

Update the meaning
Once we've got to the worst of the worst, we put our heads together to work out how much truth it holds today. One patient said the

worst thing about dying was that she'd be unable to help her son achieve his full potential and would be letting him down. But every day since her car accident, she had actually been helping her son study for an aptitude test called the 11+.

> The updated memory links the past to the present, never stopping at the worst moment.

My patient had not let her son down at all. But because terrifying memories of the car accident had flooded her mind day in day out, always stopping at the worst moment, she'd been stuck. She was unable to link today's facts to the past, unable to link to the memory that she was helping her son study daily and in no way had she let him down.

Link the new meaning to the worst moment

The updated memory links the past to the present, never stopping at the worst moment. It stops in the present day so that facts can be linked to thoughts held at the time. In this example, the updated memory captured the details of the accident and then carried on to include crucial facts: that the patient survived and that now she's helping her son study for the full-on 11+ exam.

Then what?

Make it stick

To help the updated memory stick, we link a reminder, like a photo or a physical action like a stretch, to it. It sounds unusual, but there is logic to this step.

Remember what we learned about memory? The more we recall an event, the more we'll remember it even if we change a few details along the way. Linking a reminder to the updated information helps people to remember it.

So, with their updated memory in tow, my patients then look at photos taken since the trauma or may move in such a way that proves their worst fears did not happen. My patient whose worst fears about dying linked to deeper ones about letting her son down reminded herself that these fears failed to fly. She'd recall the new information we uncovered, link it to the car crash when she talked about it then grab her phone and look at a selfie she had taken with her son after he had nailed his mock 11+ exam. Seeing a photo with her son helped the new information ('I'm alive, I'm supporting him') to cement with the memory of the car crash.

And where does the stretch come in? When people's worst fears are about being trapped and paralysed or just trapped, then stretching or moving in a way that was not possible at the time helps to strengthen the link between what they know today (no longer trapped, can walk) and what they thought at the time (trapped, can't walk). If my lady who survived her car accident had also feared being trapped, then when she updated her memory, I would have asked her to stand up and jog for a few seconds to prove to her brain that she's no longer trapped and that fears linked to being trapped no longer carry weight.

Refocus with the help of Then vs Now

When the memory pops to mind, remind yourself of your new information, then focus on how *now* is different to *then,* the time of the troublesome event.

*HOW TO MAKE TROUBLESOME MEMORIES
MORE SPONGY & LESS SPRINGY*

(When the outcome was kinder than you thought at the time)

SPOT
- Where does the memory get stuck?
- What's the worst moment?
- Ask yourself
  o What's so bad about it?
  o What would it mean if it had really happened?
  o What does it mean that it did happen?
  o What does it say about you as a person?

INVESTIGATE LIKE A DETECTIVE
- How accurate is the worst meaning?
- What information do you have now that may weaken the worst meaning?

CONNECT THE PRESENT TO THE PAST
- Link facts to the worst moments
  o If you were terrified you would die at the time, and you survived, and the worst thing about dying for you is that you would never see your kids again, link the new and true information you have now to the worst moment of the memory – 'I survived, I'm alive. I see my children every day.'

MAKE IT STICK
- Capture the new information (e.g. you survived; you see your kids) with a photo. When the memory pops to mind, remind yourself of what you know now and look at the photo

73

- Move in a way that may not have been possible at the time
  – particularly useful if fears at the time were about being
  trapped

RE-FOCUS WITH THEN VS NOW
- When the memory pops to mind, remind yourself of your
  new information, then refocus on what you can see and
  hear *now*, noting how this is different to *then*

What if the worst happened?

But what if someone's worst fear did happen? What if they were
terrified they would lose their leg and then this happened? Or
perhaps they were terrified they'd go blind and then this happened?
Or they thought their husband would leave them and he did?

Updating memories of loss and change is a little like updating
memories linked to fears that didn't happen. We spot the worst
meaning stuck to the worst moment and update it.

But how can you update a memory when the worst meaning is 'I'll
lose my legs and never be able to walk again' and then this actually
happened?

Well, let's look at this. I would be curious about the meaning of no
longer having healthy legs. So, I would be asking my typical bizarre
question: What's the worst thing about having your legs amputated? Plus, another one: What does this say about you as a person?

It's the latter question that's really key here. Usually it unveils a string
of self-deprecating thoughts, such as 'I'm different' and 'I'm defective'. To update the meaning, we put our heads together to look at
how accurate it is then spot similarities rather than differences to

other people. When someone has lost their limbs, they may look different to other people but what they value will be similar.

I also look at what has not been lost. What is the person still able to do?

Ironing out memories of injury

If or when our worst fears happen and we are badly injured, the key to ironing out this sort of memory is to uncover the painful meaning of the injury and our loss. Then we link facts to the thoughts that are fuelling feelings of inadequacy, difference and loss. It's helpful in the process to look at what we're still able to do and what dealing with our injury says about our extraordinary resolve.

Of course, this takes time. With loss, there's grief and it won't be possible to process or update what has happened right after such a significant life change. But it can come with time and effort.

When we've physically recovered and we're back in a day-to-day routine, then we can ask ourselves the tough questions:

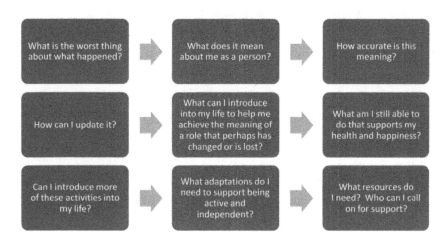

How did Joshua update his injury?

Joshua's bullet wound ripped up his right leg, robbing him of the ability to walk without aids. When Joshua's body healed as much as it was going to, he had months of gruelling rehab to learn to walk again. Gone were the days when he would frontline a humanitarian mission. He would never return to Iraq in the same capacity. He would never run on the beach with his six-year-old sister or chase her around the park in a game of hide-and-seek. But Joshua could still walk. He could still speak, think and, most dear to Joshua, he could still be helpful to other people. Joshua said the worst thing about his injury was not being able to frontline a humanitarian mission. He believed it meant he was failing his platoon. He longed to return to Iraq, to be useful and to see his friends there.

Joshua pushed through thoughts of failure hovering around his recovery, linking possibilities for success to the worst meaning of the injury.

He said he understood the medical system like never before. He knew resilience from the inside out, and how to build it in soldiers. He'd been through a physical and emotional quagmire and come out the other side, convinced he could help soldiers bounce back from extreme stress. He flipped his injury; he spotted what he could still do and ran with it, so to speak. In an upbeat telephone call, he confidently told me that . . . 'After an injury like this, you realise you may not be able to fulfil your life goals, but you realise you can still contribute to society, fulfilling a position that's different to the one you had.'

Joshua spoke at one of the meetings organised by the Tragedy Assistance Program for Survivors. About 100 grieving spouses and parents showed up. A mother's son had died in combat. His legs had to be amputated due to injury and twenty minutes later he died. Lots of questions punctuated her grief. Did he give up the will to live because he knew he'd never walk again? This woman asked Joshua if he would rather die than lose his limbs? Could her son have given up the will to live when they amputated his legs, causing him to die?

Joshua understood where this mother was coming from. He too used to think he'd rather die than have a limb amputated.

'But in those moments, when you're facing death,' he said, 'you really figure out what matters and what's important.' He told her that when he was facing death, he thought, 'Take my leg, I'll figure the rest out later'. He was more than sure that her son would have thought the same, that it was not a lack of will that killed him, but the injuries. Those few minutes in which they talked transformed her grief, from being stuck to unstuck. Joshua walked outside and crumpled with tears. Throughout his recovery, he had asked himself, 'Why did I survive? Why am I still here?' and in that moment he believed he had the answer to this question.

Joshua returned to be in charge of 130 soldiers in Iraq, championing resilience and welcoming emotional health into the unit.

Break-up

If you're going through a break-up or have recently lived through one, the memory of the relationship melt-down can pop to mind when you don't want it to, triggering gut-wrenching guilt, loss, regret, fears about the future and anger.

Break-ups are tough and have a way of seeping into your mind, keeping you stuck in your head, wishing things had been different, questioning the future and what that whole awful piece of rejection (whether you're being rejected or doing the rejecting) may mean about you as a person.

It's normal after a break-up for the other person and what happened between the two of you to pop to mind. Gradually these memories will wane, especially the more you're able to absorb yourself in creating an extraordinary life rather than trying to change the past.

Planning something fun, something that gets you out of your head, and following through with it no matter how rotten you feel offers the first breath to success and is often enough to freshen your resolve to try new activities, put yourself first and recreate your incredible life.

But how can you get going when you're longing for duvet days and another tub of Häagen-Dazs? Read Chapter V, Extraordinary Behaviours! Before then – try baking the best-ever chocolate chip cookies for your neighbour, walking briskly for seven minutes, catching a groovy class at the gym or setting an achievable but I-have-do-it task, like tidying the living room in twenty minutes or less. A morsel of achievement is enough to motivate more and bigger steps away from your couch and into the extraordinary world.

Of course, break-ups are rotten. From our lowest of lows, it's tough to see that one day we'll be okay with what happened and will have created a new, happier life for ourselves. The best way to approach break-ups when you're letting go of someone you love and can't be with (for any number of reasons such as, distance or impossible-to-live-with character traits or perhaps wildly different life goals), is to approach the loss like . . . a bereavement.

But they're not dead!

They're not dead but your romantic relationship with them is dead, dusted and gone. If you can see it this way, then you'll be more likely to give your life the full attention it deserves rather than recycling with a broken relationship.

First we spot the worst meaning of the break-up. What does it say about you as a person? You may think it means 'I'm unlovable' and 'I'll be alone forever'. Then we update the limiting belief that's holding you back from grabbing the reins of your life and galloping into your extraordinary future. Here we would tune to evidence that yes, you are lovable. Tuning to evidence that you're lovable stops you chewing over what happened and helps you tap happier times and thoughts about yourself.

This is where I get out my flashing neon hazard lights and hold up a huge sign: *Act on Facts Not Feelings*. While you may feel unlovable this does not mean you are unlovable. The facts are, of course, you are lovable, that's why you were in the relationship in the first place. The feeling is loss, sadness, gut-wrenching rejection.

It's temporary.

Remember what we've learned about troublesome memories. The key is to create continuity with the nuts and bolts of the memory, to update the meaning and link it to the present. This is important. It's tempting to slip into black-and-white thinking when it comes to rejection and loss. A happier way to move forward without heaps of self-blame or harsh criticism is to think about how you

79

can take the best part of what the person meant to you into the future.

What this means is first spotting what qualities the other person brought out in you – your playfulness? Your ability to be organised and on top of responsibilities? Then in connecting with your playful side, for example, you are connecting with the qualities that were alive in the relationship you've had to let go of. This creates a sense of continuity between the good parts of the relationship and you moving forward.

You spot what you loved about the other person then you find something (not someone!) that connects you to what you loved. Perhaps you loved their gentleness. Put aside any hurtful behaviour that may have arisen between the two of you. When you feel the gentleness of the sun trace your arms on a warm day, you are connecting with gentleness. You're experiencing for a moment that the gentleness your loved one shared is all around you. In this way, perhaps you'll feel like you connect with the very qualities you loved and had to let go of when the relationship ended. Connecting with these qualities and experiencing them around you rather than between you and your lost love can help you to feel less lonely and more capable of creating your extraordinary life.

If the relationship melt-down pops to mind, grabbing your attention, use the momentary lapse of focus as a cue to remind yourself of the updated meaning of the break-up and a cue to refocus on what you're planning today to feel wonderful.

Sometimes we painfully and shamelessly chew over the past because we feel guilty about what we did. Chewing it over is a form of torture. It's important to recognise we all make mistakes with the people we love. It's part of being human rather than saintly. Try to think about what you did that was helpful, and the reasons you made the decisions for the hurtful behaviour at the time.

Writing a letter to someone you feel you've hurt (you don't need to send it) can unleash much-needed compassion for yourself. You could also create a say-sorry-scene in your mind's eye and imagine you're saying sorry to the person you've hurt. What you saw in the last chapter is the powerful effect our images have – to the brain they're very much like real experiences. Imagining saying sorry in real time in your mind's eye is a little like saying it in real life; you'll feel brushed with relief and compassion.

When we tap compassion for ourselves, we lower our stress hormones and are much more likely to feel optimistic. Optimism helps you to problem-solve better, which is highly useful as you plan your transition across the threshold of ordinary to extraordinary.

IT'S A BREAK-UP MEMORY

LOOK AFTER YOURSELF
- Eat, wash and sleep no matter how rotten you feel
- Plan something fun that gets you out of your head and follow through with it
  - o Bake the best-ever chocolate chip cookies for your neighbour
  - o Get off the couch and out the house, walk briskly for seven minutes
  - o Catch a groovy class at the gym
  - o Set an achievable I-have-to-do-it task like 'tidy living room in twenty minutes or less'

APPROACH THE BREAK-UP LIKE A BEREAVEMENT
- They're not dead but your romantic relationship is dead, dusted and gone
- Avoid recycling with a broken relationship

SPOT
- The answers to the question
  - o What does the break-up say about you as a person?

INVESTIGATE LIKE A DETECTIVE
- How accurate is the worst meaning?
- What evidence do you have today to weaken the worst meaning?

BE CURIOUS
- What qualities did the person bring out in you?
  - o Playfulness, gentleness, being organised?
- What qualities did you love most about them?
- What captures those qualities today?

CONNECT WITH EXAMPLES OF THE QUALITIES YOU LOVED
- If you loved their gentleness, when the warmth of the sun gently traces your skin, you're connecting with gentleness and the experience of it being around you rather than between you
- If you loved their thoughtfulness, when a colleague offers a cup of tea, you're connecting with thoughtfulness around you rather than between you and your lost love

REMIND YOURSELF
- When the memory pops to mind, use it is a cue to refocus on what steps you're planning today to be extraordinary

RACKED WITH GUILT?
- Write a letter and say what you need to say – you don't need to send it
- Imagine in your mind's eye a conversation with the person where you say sorry

When do you update a memory and when do you use Then vs Now?

If a troublesome memory is popping to mind and making you feel rubbish, then you need to update it, and the sooner the better. Smoothing out the wrinkle, the worst meaning of that memory, with new information will help to make it less springy – less likely to come to mind and disrupt your focus. Spot the worst meaning, update it and bring new and true information into that worst moment. Every time that memory comes to mind, link it to information that you know now that updates the meaning. Remember what Joshua did with his memory of his injury? Or what Carina did with her memory of messing up her job interview? The troublesome memories became trouble-free when they updated the worst meaning of their memories, linking them to new and current information, which kept their memories rolling forward rather than stuck in the worst of the worst.

Once you've updated a troublesome memory, whenever it pops to mind, remind yourself of what you know now then break the links with the past. Spot all the ways *now* is different to *then*, which unhooks you from the past problem.

Of course, it's not always practical to update a troublesome memory. It may spring to mind when your boss asks for your thoughts on the company's newly designed website, or you're about to answer a question in an interview on why you're the best candidate for the job. It takes seconds to use Then vs Now and get you back on track. Use it. Spot all the ways *now* is different to *then*. This will help you to tune to what's going on in front of you rather than on what happened in the past. When you have a few minutes alone, then update the memory . . . unless using Then vs Now has already made the memory much less springy and it's coming to mind . . . well, hardly at all. There's no need to update a memory that's lost its spring. Carry on using Then vs Now until the memory is truly done and dusted and settled in the past.

How Can You Take This Forward?

This chapter has been all about memory: how the brain creates then recreates memory and how some troublesome ones keep your memory in overdrive.

To get through a troublesome memory, spot the worst meaning of the memory, update it and make it stick. Updating memories helps to settle them more smoothly with other life memories turning down rather than raising their volume.

Part of updating is spotting unhelpful beliefs that may be glued to the memory's worst moment and assessing them with the scrutiny of a detective – would the evidence you've been focusing on till now stand up in court? Then you build a new belief, one that's accurate, that holds new and true information, and you link it to the worst meaning of the worst moment of your troublesome memory.

We've all lived through events we wished we'd never had and when triggers bring those moments back to life today we need to break the link, spotting what's different to back then, so we can unhook ourselves from times of self-doubt, trauma or trouble.

Whether you're dealing with trauma, memories of self-doubt or of incredulous arguments, this chapter guides you to rework the meaning of your memory so it's rich and fluid rather than disorganised and stuck, and break the link to triggers that keep you recycling the past.

In a Nutshell

People who transition from ordinary to extraordinary clean up their memories. They rewrite the bad times, not by changing the facts of what happened but by changing the meaning of their challenging times.

Rewriting our memories is called *updating*, where we update the worst meaning of the memory.

Memories are pliable like putty. How a question is phrased, what we're feeling, how much we've slept, how we see ourselves, and whether we're better able to remember facts or stories can change a memory.

The language you use to describe your memories can help or hinder you.

It's possible to rewrite memories. It's what the brain naturally does when you remember an event.

Updating memories makes them more spongy and less springy.

Being extraordinary means breaking the link to events that fuel self-doubt.

When there's rubbish you've lived through:
1. First, recognize you got through it!
2. Flip it. What does the event say about the other people involved?
3. Break the link between *Then* and *Now*
4. Tune to evidence that supports your extraordinary belief

Then vs Now helps you to spot all the ways now is different to then, which unhooks the present from the past.

Make your troublesome memories trouble-free
  - Spot the worst meaning
  - Assess the worst of the worst with the scrutiny of a detective then update it
  - Bring new and true information into that worst moment
  - Break the link with triggers that bring the memory to mind

The prompts in the boxes in this chapter will help you to update different types of troublesome memories.

Every time the memory comes to mind, link it to information that you know now that updates the meaning. Never let the memory stop at the worst moment.

If it's not practical to update a troublesome memory, use Then vs Now first then update the memory when you have a few moments ... Unless Then vs Now has already helped the memory to settle and it's coming to mind hardly at all.

III.

Focus

In the last chapter, we looked at how to change our relationship to our memories by changing the meaning of our tough times. Updating our memories keeps them rich and fluid rather than disorganised and stuck, and stops our focus from being pulled to the past. In this chapter, we'll look at how to keep our focus more fully in the here and now, and why it's crucial to get out of our head and into the task at hand.

Imagine you need heart surgery. How would you feel if you discovered that your surgeon would be taking phone calls in the middle of the surgery? Or snacking on a burger while searching for the scalpel? Or glancing at a film playing on a screen above your head while trying to locate your aorta? How confident would you be in this surgeon's ability to perform the operation safely?

Whenever our focus is divided with competing stimuli (such as different sounds, smells, tastes, images, thoughts and desires) we have a harder time finishing up a task and doing it well. Things will take longer and we're more likely to do a sloppy job.

Leading an extraordinary life requires that we say 'yes' to what we value and 'no' to what we don't, especially distractions during the time we've allocated to our worthy projects. We must become disciplined in creating environments that allow us to focus. When we're absorbed in what we're doing, we're less likely to feel the angst and stress of our problems. We're less likely to tie ourselves up in knots and we're much more likely to get things done to bring our worthy projects to fruition.

People who transition from ordinary to extraordinary with trauma as their catalyst choose to focus on what they can do rather than on what they have lost. They also develop their attention muscle. They have to. Trauma gives people first-hand experience that time really is limited. They come to realise that they don't have endless years to will their dreams into reality. They've seen that lives can change in a second. So, they optimise their time and one of the ways they do this is by learning to focus efficiently without distraction.

In this chapter, we'll look at helpful and unhelpful attention; the latter keeps anxiety going, whether it's anxiety linked to PTSD or anxiety linked to health worries, panic or public speaking. We'll also look at how to focus attention, a much-needed skill to thrive. In this day and age when the brain is drawn to distraction, becoming more focused requires discipline. We'll learn from Mary who had a family to care for when she received news of a life-threatening health condition. Mary focused on what she *could* do, what she had *not* lost, and she trained her mind to focus during her short breaks from chemo and radiotherapy. She subsequently built a programme to support men and women to recover from aggressive cancer, a life-changing tool for people who had little time to wait.

A bit much to swallow

Paramedics, firefighters and police officers see a lot of suffering and are at risk of becoming sick with severe stress like PTSD. So, when I begin teaching them tools to improve their resilience, I first ask them to . . . swallow.

I make it tough so I can prove a point. I ask them to concentrate hard on swallowing, to focus all of their attention on making sure they swallow, and whilst focusing on swallowing, I ask them to spot three colours in the room.

Then I ask my emergency workers to clear their heads and use their full attention to do one thing, and that one thing is to spot three different colours in the room. That's all they have to do. Find three different colours in the room with their full attention.

Then we look at the differences. Which situation felt more tense? Which was easier? Focusing on our throats and finding colours or just focusing on finding colours?

What does this tell us about attention? In which situation were the emergency workers more likely to achieve effortlessly what they were meant to? When they were focusing hard on the sensation of swallowing, making sure they swallowed and at the same time searching for three colours? Or, just finding three colours?

They much preferred and were faster at finding three colours when that's all they had to do. Focusing hard and long on swallowing made it more difficult.

I sometimes follow this up by asking them to go home, plop themselves in front of the television, switch on the news and focus on their body, on where there's tension and to give those areas a lot of attention. At the same time, they're to follow the news for two minutes. Then they must clear their head and focus on the news for a full two minutes, only the news.

What do they discover?

They take in a lot more information when their attention is out of their head, out of their body and in the world. They're much more likely to feel comfortable and to get accurate information about what's going on.

What I teach emergency workers is the difference between helpful and unhelpful attention.

> Self-focused attention is attention that has flipped inwards to our thoughts, feelings, fears or sensations in our body.

1. Helpful and Unhelpful Attention

Unhelpful attention is focus that's gone inside ourselves to our thoughts, feelings and fears, or sensations in our body like our heart rate. When our attention is inside ourselves, our minds are distracted from experiencing what's going on and we're more likely to get caught up in what we're thinking and feeling.

Attention that's flipped inwards is called *self-focused attention*. When our attention is self-focused, we're inattentive to what's actually happening. Self-focused attention makes it difficult to take in the environment and therefore gives us misleading information – information based on what we may be feeling rather than on facts or evidence. It will make you feel more self-conscious and less at ease compared to attention that's out of your head.

Self-focused attention is at the crux of most psychological problems like depression, anxiety, worry and stress. I can't think of one psychological problem where self-focused attention is not part of the problem.

Feeling downright blue

When people are depressed, they are drawn to their thinking, which often includes a string of self-deprecating descriptors ... 'I'm a failure', 'I'm no good at what I do', 'I always get things wrong'. These thoughts are normal from time to time, but when people are depressed, they struggle to break free from this kind of thinking and their focus stays in their head.

Research shows that when people focus on unhappy thoughts, they're more likely to remember the bad times. So, not only does the focus on unhappy thoughts keep them blue, while they're doing it, they're more likely to remember unhappy times. It's pretty hard to break free from feeling blue when attention is in your head recycling sad thoughts and bad times.

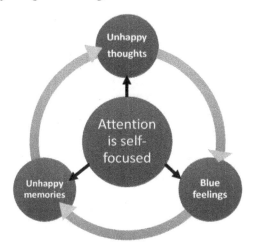

What about anxiety?

At the crux of anxiety problems like social anxiety or health anxiety or panic or excessive worry is unhelpful attention. And whilst stuck memories are at the crux of PTSD, unhelpful attention has a significant role in keeping traumatic stress going.

Feeling jittery talking to others

The effects of self-focused attention can be seen most clearly in social anxiety.

When people are terrified of chit-chat with strangers or of speaking their mind in a meeting or of speaking in public, they tend to switch from helpful to unhelpful attention. Suddenly, they're focused on how hot or shaky or terrified they feel. Their attention is self-focused. They're giving their body and their fears their full attention, which makes it harder to do what they're meant to be doing: thinking of things to say and saying them.

Giving your fears a lot of attention makes them feel like they're more likely to come true, which will keep your attention in your head and body rather than in the outside world noticing how people are really responding to you.

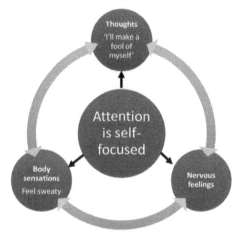

Reining attention into your body and your head, where your thinking sits, will make you more uncomfortable and self-conscious when you're trying to speak. It has another consequence, too. While you're focusing on yourself, just like in the swallowing exercise, it's much harder to take in what's going on around you. You're not going to spot the encouraging nod your boss makes. You won't notice that the colleagues you're chatting to are smiling in agreement with you.

Even if you're fairly relaxed talking with others, if you turn your attention inwards so that it is self-focused, you'll instantly feel anxious. I carried out a fun study with my colleague, David M. Clark, who is widely known for developing cognitive therapy for panic and social anxiety disorders, the most effective treatment for these problems.

We gave people false feedback about how anxious they were. I wired up over seventy students who were low or high in social anxiety with a small vibrating device which I programmed to go off eight times during a short conversation. A third of the students were told when the device vibrated that we were picking up signs of anxiety and another third were told we were picking up signs of being relaxed. I showed these students their fake heart-rate traces to make the feedback more believable. The final third of students were told to just ignore the device – we said we were testing its comfort level.

We found that it didn't matter if people were high or low in social anxiety, we could make them anxious simply by making them switch their attention inwards. Making people focus on themselves and on possible signs of anxiety made them anxious and they were more likely to believe they performed poorly.

But there was no difference between the high and low social anxiety groups in the number of vibrations they detected or in the extent to which they believed the feedback. People who were low in social anxiety at the outset and who had been told that the vibrating device was picking up signs of anxiety were experimentally made to behave like patients with social anxiety disorder, in that they were made to shift their attention away from the conversation to themselves. As a result, they became socially anxious for the duration of the eight-minute conversation they had.

Turning to health anxiety

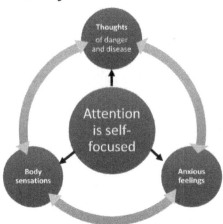

People who suffer from health anxiety exacerbate their fears with self-focused attention. They're often focused on thoughts of danger and disease and sensations in their bodies. When we focus on our body, like our throat and how we're swallowing, we notice things that we otherwise wouldn't and it's common to string together various sensations, concluding they're symptoms of disease. One route to recovering from health anxiety is learning to break free from focusing on danger, and instead, shifting attention to the task at hand.

And worry

People who worry excessively find their attention is in their head, not in the moment. When we give our worries a lot of attention, it feels like they're more likely to come true.

Post-traumatic stress

People who have got through the other side of a trauma and are dealing with PTSD tend to give their fears a lot of attention, which splits their attention between their head and the outside world. If they're feeling anxious, they'll be more likely to look for signs of danger when they're out and about, which has the paradoxical effect of increasing rather than decreasing their anxiety.

Breaking free

Breaking free from anxiety, worry, depression and stress reactions, like PTSD, requires many steps and one of the most important ones is developing a bulletproof capacity to focus on the task at hand – to spot when attention has turned inwards and to use the awareness to refocus on what is happening in the here and now.

People who transition from ordinary to extraordinary with or without trauma as their catalyst have discovered the link between focus and feelings. They know that the risk of bad things happening does not change with a bad event. But what is at risk of shifting is what we focus on. Focus on avoiding danger and you keep your mind on threat, fuelling frightened feelings and stay-put behaviour. Clearly, it matters what you focus on.

> Externally focused attention is the kind of attention that's out of your head and in the world.

Helpful attention

Helpful attention is the kind of attention that's out of your head and in the world.

Attention we give to the task at hand, to other people and to what is going on moment by moment is externally focused attention. It simply means our attention is out of our head. When we are really absorbed in something, such as a good book, exercise or demanding tasks like writing a cover letter for a new job, our attention is externally focused – absorbed in the task at hand. This kind of attention is linked to feeling more upbeat and at ease and to greater feelings of well-being.

Early in the 1980s, psychologist Mihaly Csikszentmihalyi had people record how they felt and what they were doing in real time in response to random prompts throughout the day. His team discovered that people were most satisfied when they were absorbed in the task at hand, particularly when they were absorbed in something that was challenging enough to be stimulating, but not so challenging that it was frustrating.

Why is self-focused attention unhelpful?

It makes you feel self-conscious
Self-focused attention can make you feel self-conscious and uncomfortable around other people. Switching attention inwards when you're speaking in a meeting, calling a client, walking into a room whilst others are seated or even performing a skill like driving will make you feel like you're the centre of everyone's attention, which could affect how you come across.

It makes it harder to concentrate
When your attention has shifted inwards, it's more difficult to concentrate, which means it will be tougher to finish an email, write a cover letter, read a book, follow the news or your favourite Netflix series.

It gives you misleading information

When we are focusing on ourselves it can feel like everyone is focusing on us as well, which can make us feel like the centre of everyone's attention. Switching our attention from ourselves to the outside world helps us to realise that not everyone else is paying attention to us as well.

It's unrewarding

When we're focused on ourselves, we're not absorbed in the task at hand and so we're much less likely to feel happy and fulfilled. In fact, we will feel quite the opposite. We're much more likely to feel stressed, anxious and uncertain.

Where's your attention?

Is your attention in or out? Self-focused attention takes you inwards to your thoughts, your feelings, your body and your worries. When our attention is self-focused, we take in little accurate information. Just like when my emergency workers focused all their attention on their bodies, their attention was inwards, and they found it tough to follow the news.

Externally focused attention takes you out of your head and into the world.

Key signs of self-focused attention are:

o Feeling anxious, uncomfortable or self-conscious

o Being caught up in thoughts or questions that have no obvious answers

o Monitoring how you are coming across to other people

o Being over-aware of physical sensations, such as a racing heart or feeling shaky

A key question to ask to help you spot self-focused attention is: Am I noticing the world around me? Notice when your attention has shifted to yourself – to your feelings, your worries or how you are coming across. This is a sign that your attention has gone inwards and is a cue for you to refocus your attention to the outside world.

Mary's Story

Mary is a white English woman who converted from Catholicism to Islam in her twenties after her brother's suicide. She married and raised four children, guiding them gently but firmly through their teenage years. Her job as a mother of four was made more difficult by the unusual challenges she faced as a white Muslim woman in middle-class Britain, as well as the loss of her mother to Alzheimer's. While being there for her children during their tumultuous teens, she forgot to care for herself. She discovered a lump in her breast and ignored it for an entire year. When it was 10 cm in size, she was whisked into surgery where a radical double mastectomy was performed. At the time, Mary declined minimal reconstructive surgery, which would have enabled future plastic surgery to have been more natural-looking. Mary simply wanted the cancer out of her body as quickly as possible without complicating her recovery.

After surgery, she had a year of chemotherapy, abandonment by her husband, six months of radiotherapy, and the death of her mother. Against all odds, Mary recovered physically and emotionally. She regained her spirit and her drive. Delving deep into her experience, she asked herself tough questions. She realised that she had allowed her cancer to become almost fatal because she had not cared for herself; she had been unwilling or unable to extend the compassion and kindness she so readily extended to her family to herself. She realised unless she did extend kindness and care to herself, she would lose her life, and that taking time to care for herself also modelled how she would want her children to care for themselves as adults. Mary spotted a link between feeling stronger with recovery and the kindness, support and advocacy she received whilst ill.

Mary's insights inspired her to develop a programme where she and other people she trained offer time, advocacy and care to men and women newly diagnosed with cancer. She speaks to their families and works out ways to ensure they are well nourished with knowledge, compassion and food. She accompanies her clients to their medical appointments, asking the tough questions they cannot ask or that they forget to ask. And she shares the latest scientific findings and inspiring stories of other people's recovery, instilling hope and health in many battling with cancer.

Here's a useful exercise you could try which shows just how tough it is to get accurate information when your attention is self-focused.

Have you ever walked into a team meeting, busy restaurant or café, or buzzing party and felt self-conscious?

If you've answered yes to this question, more than likely you were self-focused at the time. Have a go with the exercise below. Even if you're confident walking into a packed room where everyone is already seated, you may still like to try this exercise. It's eye- opening to experience how self-focused attention gives misleading information.

Step One: Think of a situation where there will be quite a few people, such as a team meeting, busy café or restaurant, or a packed party.

Step Two: Go into the situation, look down and initially focus most of your attention on yourself and how you think you are coming across to other people.

Step Three: Once you have focused on yourself for half a minute or so and are feeling self-conscious, make a prediction about how many people might be staring at you and how they will be looking, for example, 'I feel that most people will be staring at me, not just glancing in my direction, and some will be giving me a weird look. I believe this 80 per cent.' Once you've made your prediction, look up and check it out.

Step Four: Once you have completed this exercise, make a note of what you found.

Here's what one of my emergency workers wrote:

Situation	Prediction	Experiment	Outcome	Learning
Go into the crew room when it is busy.	Everyone will turn and stare at me as I walk in. I believe this will happen 90%.	Initially focus on myself and don't look at other people. Think how I might appear to others and estimate how many people might be looking at me. Then look up and around and note how many people are actually looking at me.	I felt uncomfortable focusing on myself in the busy crew room. I looked down and thought 90% of my colleagues were staring at me. That's how it felt. But when I looked up and around, I noticed no one was really looking at me. Everyone seemed to be enjoying their conversations with each other. Someone vaguely looked up as I came in but wasn't really paying attention to me.	When I focus my attention on myself, that is, when my attention is self-focused, it makes me feel self-conscious and gives me misleading information. I'll use this feeling as a cue to look up and around and shift my attention out of my head.

Attention Training: the key to getting out of your head

The steps to train your attention:

1. Notice when your attention has gone inwards. The most common signs are feeling self-conscious or being caught up in your thinking.

2. Refocus on what you can see and hear.

3. Look up and around and notice where you are and who you may be with.

4. If your attention wanders back to yourself, give yourself a break and refocus on what you can see and hear until you're reabsorbed in the task at hand.

You can try this several times a day.

Attention and problem-solving

While it is helpful to give problems our attention so we can solve them, self-focused attention for long periods of time can cause our problems to grow, just like focusing on your throat makes swallowing more difficult.

If you have a problem that needs your attention, it is more helpful to set aside time to problem-solve with *practical thinking* than to think about it on and off all day.

Practical thinking is also called 'How' thinking. It takes into account specific details like what, when, where and how a situation happened. It includes questions like: *How can I move forward? How can I break this down into smaller steps? What is the first step I can take?*

There's more on practical thinking in Chapter VI, Get Out of Your Head with Helpful Thinking Habits.

How Mary shifted attention

Mary felt self-conscious about her body during and after her recovery. She regretted declining the minimal reconstructive surgery at the time of her mastectomy. When she turned her attention inwards, focusing her attention on her body, she felt unattractive, regretful and instantly self-conscious. Mary learned to spot these feelings and use them as a cue to switch her attention from her body to the outside world, looking up and around. When she walks into a consulting room, a patient's home, a hospital waiting room, she walks with her head held high, focusing on what she can see and hear. What she notices and what comforts her is that people are rarely staring at her and if people do look at her, she looks for the kindness in their expression.

Mary was offered reconstructive surgery a year after her recovery. At the start of her cancer treatment, she thought for sure she would have it, but with a year of focusing externally under her belt and the rewarding work she was undertaking, she declined the surgery, informing the hospital she believed it would be kinder to her body to avoid what she now considered to be an unnecessary surgery.

2. What About Mind-wandering?

When our heads are in the clouds, our focus has flown far away from the task at hand. When our minds wander away from the task at hand, we take our attention into our heads, our thinking. Mind-wandering is self-focused attention and it has some interesting knock-on effects, mostly of the unhelpful sort.

Research early in the 1980s found a link between being fully absorbed in the task at hand and feeling fulfilled. We often assume we'll be most happy chilling on the couch, feet up, our minds perusing the plot of our favourite Netflix series whilst staying on the beat of our WhatsApp messages. But Csikszentmihalyi's findings challenged popular wisdom. People felt happiest when they were fully absorbed in something worthwhile and challenging, not when they were on the couch relaxing.

Following on from this with more sophisticated technology using iPhones, Matt Killingsworth studied over 15,000 people, pushing notifications to sample over 650,000 random moments in their days, collecting data on what they were doing and how they were feeling. He asked: How do you feel on a scale from very bad to very good? What are you doing? Are you thinking about something other than what you are currently doing? Is the topic of those thoughts pleasant, neutral or unpleasant?

The results were eye-opening. We are almost as distracted as we are focused. People are thinking about something other than what they are currently doing 47 per cent of the time. We're most distracted when we're having a shower or brushing our teeth. This probably fits with your experience at the start and end of your day. When we're working, we're distracted and mind-wandering 50 per cent of the time. When we're exercising we're distracted about 40 per cent of the time. We're least distracted when we're having sex, where our minds wander only 10 per cent of the time. In every activity other than sex, people are mind-wandering at least 30 per cent of the time.

In this study, people were much less happy when they were mind-wandering than when they were focused on the task at hand, even if the task was commuting. People don't like commuting to work; it's one of the least enjoyable activities but people are much happier when they're focused only on their commute than when their mind is wandering. Killingsworth and his team found the pattern held true for every single activity they measured, including the least enjoyable.

Mind-wandering preceded feeling blue rather than the other way around. This means that mind-wandering, or lack of focus, makes us blue. They speculated that the reason mind-wandering makes people so unhappy is that when our minds wander they wander to our worries, anxieties and regrets. Fodder for feeling low.

But a much smaller study of only twenty-four people found the opposite: that feeling blue led to mind-wandering. The researchers pushed six notifications to people a day, asking them to note if they were mind-wandering and what their mood had been like fifteen minutes earlier. Then fifteen minutes later they were asked a series of questions on their phone about their mood in that moment. Sadness seemed to precede mind-wandering. Mind-wandering only predicted feeling worse if the content was negative.

Ageing cells

Mind-wandering has also been linked to accelerated ageing. Not only will it make you blue, it could age you. Elissa Epel and colleagues studied the potential link between telomere length and mind-wandering in healthy women. Telomeres are the caps at the end of chromosomes, which shorten with age, stress and when cells divide. Telomere length is a proxy measure for biological ageing. They found that the tendency to mind-wander was linked to shorter telomeres even when they took levels of stress into account, meaning that mind-wandering is linked to ageing over and above the effects of stress.

Mind-wandering makes us less gritty and more likely to give up

Researchers in Canada defined grit as being able to sustain interest and effort towards long-term goals. They found that people more likely to mind-wander in everyday life were less likely to stick to their goals. They were less gritty. What this means is that you'll be more likely to achieve your goals if you can sustain your focus.

Can we focus all the time?

The short answer is . . . nope. We can't focus all the time. It seems that our attention has a cap. We can certainly focus a lot more than the 53 per cent of the time that we do. But it's important to take breaks from focus. It actually improves our attention.

You may be familiar with the 2008 study where people were split into two groups and one group walked through a beautiful wooded path in a tree sanctuary for almost an hour whilst the other group walked through the busy city of Michigan for the same length of time. Both groups were then given a challenging concentration task – backwards digit span. This is where a string of numbers is read out, increasing in length, and you have to recite them to the examiner backwards. So, 4 – 1 must be cited back as 1 – 4. Easy when there are two digits, but it gets pretty tough pretty quickly and you can be certain you won't do well if your mind is wandering.

What the researchers found is that the folk who had a lovely stroll in the tree sanctuary before the test did 20 per cent better than the folk who navigated the city streets first. It led them to conclude that our capacity to focus is finite and that walking through busy streets taxes our attention with second-by-second decisions, such as when to walk around people, when to cross the street, how to cross the street and so on. The attention-taxing task of navigating the city streets zapped people's capacity to focus in a later memory test, whereas walking through nature allowed people to break from focus to observe rather than direct their attention to navigate. The break in their directed attention capacity helped them to perform better on a later task that required their full attention.

What this means is that taking some time out in an undemanding space, like a park, helps you to focus later on.

But I get all my creative ideas when my mind wanders!

Hot on the heels of this fascinating research were a burgeoning of studies aiming to spot when and in what conditions mind-wandering may deliver some benefits.

Finally, in 2012, Benjamin Baird and colleagues found something – mind-wandering during a simple task like spotting whether a number is even or odd seemed to lead to more creative problem-solving. They gave 145 students a two-minute creativity test, asking them to come up with unusual uses for everyday objects like a tin can or a paperclip. Some students were then allowed to rest, some were given a demanding task requiring them to memorise whether or not a number that had flashed briefly on a screen was odd or even, and others were given a non-demanding task requiring them to spot whilst looking at the flashing number whether it was odd or even. Other students were not given any task or rest period. Then all students repeated the creativity test with the same objects plus two new ones. The researchers found that students in the non-demanding task that encouraged mind-wandering came up with more novel and creative uses for everyday objects when retested. Their performance improved on the previously encountered problem. So, it is possible that mind-wandering may help creativity. At least, it seems to help students discover novel uses for objects like paperclips and tin cans.

In 2013, Michael Franklin and colleagues revealed another potential benefit of mind-wandering. If you mind-wander to an interesting topic, you'll feel a boost in mood. So, if you can't focus on the task at hand, at least think about something interesting.

It matters how you focus

We saw earlier in this chapter that it matters what you focus on. When we're focused on our thoughts, feelings, fears and sensations, our attention has gone inwards and we're more likely to feel anxious or sad, distracted and unable to take in accurately what's happening right in front of us. We saw that attention that's gone inwards, or self-focused attention, has a key role in keeping depression, anxiety and PTSD going.

It clearly matters what you focus on. But it also matters *how* you focus. We saw that mind-wandering – when our attention leaves the task at hand and flies to the clouds – is linked to mostly harmful effects, thwarting our attempts to reach our goals. When multiple tasks and mind-wandering threaten to spread our attention thin, how best do we keep focus?

3. How to Fortify Your Focus

How we pilot our attention has changed over the years and some might say we are far more distractible than ever before. We stockpile devices and apps to facilitate productivity and connect us to the pulse of our work, news, interests and our friends' lives and the lives of people we've never met and people we'll never meet. We have endless opportunities for push notifications or other communications to break our focus. Even if we switch off our phones, when a piece of work gets tough, it's tempting to break for an online stroll with social media. What this does is reinforce our mind's behaviour of turning attention away from the task at hand rather than sticking it out, seeing it through and wrapping it up. We've become addicted to distraction. Continually breaking focus, like any bad habit, is tough to overcome.

People who transition from ordinary to extraordinary have discovered how to focus without distraction. They understand that their time is limited, and they use it wisely to bring their goals to fruition. Below are tried and tested methods for fortifying your focus, many of which Mary used on her transition from ordinary to extraordinary.

Welcome boring tasks

Take opportunities to seek out boring work rather than distract yourself from it. The digital age has brought many benefits and advances; one of the side effects has been instant distraction for a mind that's struggling with boring work. There you are with good intentions set, working on some tough emails, delivering some feedback sensitively written and it's, well, frankly, boring. Your mind wanders to dinner and you wonder if there's a more delicious way to roast beets and onions than the one that's just popped to mind. Your fingers do the walking and next thing you're online scrolling down the Google-searched recipes. That email?! What email?

Every time you break from focus, you teach your mind to become a master distractor and you reward the behaviour with the internet surf.

How long can you focus before you give in to a Google search or a social media update or a quick check of emails or a glance at your phone? That length of time, those seconds or minutes, is your modern-day focus. People who transition from ordinary to extraordinary can focus for hours on their projects. They know with every cell in their body that time is limited, and they've trained their minds to focus so they can bring their projects to fruition sooner rather than later. No longer will they tempt fate and delay bringing their dreams into reality. They realise our tomorrows may not be our todays, so they make the most of the time they allocate to their worthy projects when they have that time. Mary had people dying of cancer relying on her capacity to extend their last few days with her compassion and proactive approach. She learned to focus with precision. You too can overcome the urge to give in to distraction.

Take the focus fitness test

Next time you're faced with a task that requires focus, like writing an email or a report, number crunching data or writing a press release, take note of how long you focus before you check email, the net, your phone or social media. Whatever that number is, that's your base length of focus you'll be working to improve.

How?

Immediately double it. And make that your target focus. When you can repeatedly focus for that length of time, double it again until you can focus without distraction for twenty-five minutes. When there's something boring to get through, welcome the opportunity to practise focusing without giving in to distraction. Since most jobs have some pretty dull tasks linked to them, you're sure to get a lot of practice flexing your focus. Savour them. The more you practise, the more you'll be able to focus on your extraordinary projects.

You can also train your mind to live without your phone and hence the net and social media for a set period of time every day. You could start by giving yourself a phone break of thirty minutes a day and increase the length of time. Giving yourself a break from checking your phone will weaken the desire to phone check when you're working on something boring. The weaker the desire to check out while you're checking in, the stronger you'll make your focus.

Train with the attention gym

Give your attention a workout. One exercise I offer my clients is attention training from in to out. It is a technique originally used in cognitive therapy for social anxiety developed by David M. Clark. I give my clients four simple tasks and ask them to experience each one with self- or externally focused attention. We start with sounds. To conjure up self-focused attention, I ask them to close their eyes and call to mind a worry and to focus all their attention on that worry, to really think about it. Whilst focusing on that worry, I give them another task. I ask them to name two sounds they can hear. When they've got two sounds, I ask them to clear their head and to focus on only one thing and that one thing is to find two sounds. We do this a few times.

Then I ask them to open their eyes and we repeat similar steps for finding colours, differences in shade and light, and then music. I play an upbeat tune and with their attention focused on a worry, really thinking about a worry, I ask them to spot two instruments in the tune they're enjoying. When they've got this, I ask them to clear their mind. I play another upbeat tune and ask them to spot two instruments.

We follow up the exercise chatting about which was easier – finding sounds, colours, shadows and instruments with self-focused attention or with externally focused attention.

With the feeling of externally focused attention under their belt, I send them home to practise shifting their attention over the next week. Their homework is to notice what they can see and hear for three minutes a day as they walk to the shop or the bus stop. When they listen to music, their job is to focus on each instrument or the vocals for the whole song. We start out with small steps and gradually move this to chats with other people, where their task is to focus on the other person, what they're saying and how they look. When they spot their own focus is moving back inwards to their thoughts and fears, they're tasked to use this awareness as a cue to shift their attention back out of their head and into the world. In this way, they train their attention to be out of their head for increasing lengths of time.

Being able to focus on what they can see and hear – what they're observing – helps people to focus when it's time to work on their worthy projects. They're much less likely to give attention to every thought, worry or feeling that pops up unrelated to the task at hand. Practising externally focused attention strengthens their attention muscle.

You can try this too. Next time you're walking to the shop, your car or the bus stop, spot what you can see and hear. When anything other than what you can see and hear pops into your mind, such as your to-do list, whether or not you'll beat the morning traffic, and other thoughts screaming for your attention, use these thoughts as a cue to refocus on what you can see and hear. Not only will you strengthen your attention muscle, you'll also feel calmer, which will help to focus you more effectively on the things that matter, your worthy projects.

Clean up attention residue with the pressure of time

Have you ever sent an email, then started to reply to another while still thinking about the one you just fired off? Perhaps you even interrupted writing your next reply to reread the email you just sent? Or perhaps you made a snack after you'd sent a bunch of emails only to be thinking about your well-crafted replies as you plopped a splodge of chutney on your cheese toastie.

If this sounds familiar, then you'll know first-hand that finishing a task is not enough to stop thinking about it. Some of your attention will be stuck in the past task. This is called *attention residue*, when a morsel of your attention is still on a task in the past. When this happens, you'll perform less well on the next entry on your to-do list.

A typical work day involves a lot of switching from one task to the next – from meetings to answering telephone calls to replying to emails and perhaps to writing reports or analysing data. People need to stop thinking about one task to immerse themselves fully in the next one to perform well. But Sophie Leroy, a business professor at University of Minnesota, discovered that although it helps to complete a task fully before embarking on another, it's not enough to stop us from thinking about it. Even if we finish one task, our performance on the next will be affected if we have attention residue.

So, what can you do to unstick your attention from the past?

In a cool experiment, Sophie was able to demonstrate that what helps to unstick our attention is pressure. Time pressure. She had students come into the lab and complete some tasks, beginning with word puzzles for five minutes. Everyone was required to give one-word answers to clues like 'it follows ginger', 'it precedes berry', 'it precedes up', and so on.

Depending on the instructions, Sophie was able to make the task achievable or not. Some students were required to solve all seventeen clues with thirteen words in five minutes, which was achievable. Other students were required to solve the seventeen clues with five words in five minutes, which was unachievable. Sophie told the students that completion of the task predicted intelligence so that they'd be motivated to finish the task. Whilst all students had five minutes to work on the word puzzles, Sophie manipulated the experience of time pressure. Some students were told that five minutes was not a lot of time and they had to work as fast as they could. They also heard an audio recording counting down the minutes in the background, 'four minutes left', 'three minutes left', and so on, until the final 'time is up' message blared.

Other students had no such time pressure. They were told that five minutes was enough to complete the task and to work at their own pace. These students heard no audio recording of minutes remaining in the background.

Then the students completed their next task, which was to review four CVs in five minutes. After they read the CVs, Sophie surprised them with a memory test. They were given blank CVs and asked to write as many ideas as they could remember about each CV. They were asked to stop only when they could no longer remember anything else from the CVs. Then they were given a job description and asked to indicate which candidate they preferred for the position.

Performance on the CV task was assessed as the total number of accurate ideas that a person remembered from the four CVs. Sophie found that students who finished the word puzzles performed better on the memory test of CVs than people who didn't finish the word puzzles. She also found that students working under high time pressure in the word puzzle task performed better on the CV test than students who had worked under low pressure in the word puzzle task. Her study supports the idea that task performance suffers when a prior task is unfinished. Performance also suffers when people have completed the prior task under low time pressure. When people have completed the prior task under high time pressure their subsequent task performance is much better.

To mop up attention residue and unstick your mind from the past task, you have to set yourself time limits to finish up what you're working on, whether that's ten emails in ten minutes or finish prepping a presentation in sixty minutes. Giving a time limit and sticking to it forces you to work under pressure and improves your focus from one task to the next.

Plan and plan again

We saw in Chapter I, Vision, and you'll see in Chapter V, Extraordinary Behaviours, that planning ahead is essential to transition from ordinary to extraordinary. It's a simple tool backed up by loads of science, some of which has come out of my lab.

Making a plan in the evening for the next day and including an enjoyable activity in that plan improves well-being. It's also an essential step in improving your focus.

Plan every minute of your work day in half-hour chunks and use the plan as a schedule to guide you, revamping and recreating it through the day, especially when you discover that you've wildly underestimated how long it takes to reply to emails, draft your boss's letter, or write up your project results.

Planning ahead works because it moves routine decision-making to the night before, which frees up mental energy to tackle demanding tasks the following day. It also improves focus because you soon realise that, seriously, you've spent twenty minutes on one email, which can only mean one thing: your mind was wandering. So, the plan helps you get clearer on mind-wandering and with clarity you can rein your attention back in to finish the tasks at hand.

Check your Vitamin D

Vitamin D is essential to helping you think and concentrate, and two things happen as you age. The first is that it gets harder to absorb Vitamin D from the sun. Your skin is, well, older and tougher. The reality is older skin struggles to soak up the good stuff to support your brain. But this leads to the next point, which is that our responsibilities tend to increase as we age. This usually means we get out in the sun a lot less, even when it does shine. Most of my patients are deficient in Vitamin D, which makes focus a lot more challenging. So, when you have a moment, get your Vitamin D checked and at the very least, take a multivitamin with Vitamin D in it. Unless you live in the Caribbean and your job is sailing boats to swim with dolphins, you may well need a Vitamin D boost. Worth checking.

Resist the temptation to give in when the going gets tough

Hard work is . . . well, hard. Resist the temptation to switch off or space out as soon as your mind draws a blank at the blank page, the complicated theorem, the hard-to-follow email, the code that hasn't worked, the report on product performance, or whatever other conundrum has come up in your work.

Stay with the hard stuff. Spacing out, watching your mind wander away to your phone or the clouds, teaches your brain to give up when challenged. It will be much harder to solve the challenge if you've reinforced behaviour that allows you to instantly switch off in response to the tough stuff. Stick it out. You'll find if you can keep going, thinking through the hard stuff, keep working with it, you'll get better at it and you'll solve it much faster than if you give way to breaks and distraction.

Remember Csikszentmihalyi's findings – it is actually rewarding to stretch your mind. People are happiest when they are fully absorbed in a demanding and worthwhile task. But you only discover this if you stick it out and force your mind to stretch its focus.

Change your attention filter

We all have an attention filter, which works like a spotlight, orientating our focus towards helpful or unhelpful stuff. People who transition from ordinary to extraordinary have updated their memories and beliefs, so their filter highlights evidence to support success. They can get on and focus because they don't have an inner voice screaming that they can't do it, highlighting every setback as evidence for failure. Self-focused attention with a spotlight focus on how you may fail is not going to improve your attention to the task at hand. If your memories or beliefs are guiding you

116

to spot ways you *can't* rather than ways you *can* succeed, then you may need to update them. Chapter I, Vision, and Chapter II, Fluid Memory, can help with this.

Being extraordinary means unhooking the present from events that fuel self-doubt. The more you can break the link between the present and the past, the more you'll be able to focus on your worthy projects unencumbered by anything that's happened before today.

Start out small and get bigger

Focus for a few minutes – perhaps three minutes, on something demanding. Set yourself the challenge, for instance, 'Reply to two emails in three minutes.' Achieved it? Reward yourself with a lengthier requirement to focus. When you can get up to twenty-five minutes of focus, reward yourself with a five-minute break – a tea, biscuit, stretch or brief internet search – then get back to work. Soon you'll be able to move on to larger attention-sized shoes, focusing for longer stretches and the uninterrupted stretches will be your reward. Until then, small shoes, small steps.

Work out what your go-to is and delay getting there

What's your go-to when you're working on something hard, like starting a new report, writing code or a sensitive email? One of my client's go-to methods is sleep: she instantly feels tired and has the urge to nap when faced with a tough task that requires her full focus. Another client goes to his phone and plays games.

What's your go-to when you're faced with something tough and you're stumped with an urge to give up? When we give in to our go-to rather than stick with our focus, we strengthen our neural network linking focus to giving up. What this means is that our brains learn that as soon as we need to focus, we also need to give up. As strong as the urge is to turn your attention away from what's hard or boring or both, use your mightiest will to stick with it even if only for thirty seconds in the beginning and then for longer stretches. You need to rewire your brain so that you are reinforcing focus rather than reinforcing giving up on focus.

Compassion for the overwhelming

When faced with tough work – writing a report from scratch, translating stock market trends into simple English, writing or spotting mistakes in code, or writing a sales pitch for a new product or house – we know before we even begin that they're challenging and we're probably already gritting our teeth, tense with this knowledge, which can make it hard to focus. So, first, get cosy with compassion. Compassion lowers stress hormones and without those molecules running riot through your body, you'll be more able to focus. Give yourself a gentle nudge – you can do it, of course you can. Before you start, picture clearly in your mind's eye two people who really appreciate you. Then remind yourself that you're in a safe place in your home or at work and that you have what you need to get going on the task at hand. Then take a few deep breaths and get going. Extending a bit of kindness to yourself can help you to feel calmer, more optimistic and better able to problem-solve the task you face with your full focus.

Quit multi-tasking

Skip the temptation to do many things at once. Multi-tasking is not a good thing when it comes to productivity. It affects the quality of your work and is a waste of time. Do not take a phone call while also typing an email. Focus on one thing until you finish it. If you've got ten phone calls to make, block off time and make your calls. If you've got fourteen emails to reply to, block off time and focus on writing your emails. A presentation you have to prep from scratch? Block off time and do it and only it. Focusing on one thing until completion wipes out attention residue and leads to better-quality work.

Spot your productivity peak

There are times during the day when you'll find you focus more easily and it varies from person to person. It can also change across your lifetime due to changes in hormones (adolescent peak productivity is unlikely to be between 8 and 10 a.m.), schedules (consistently full schedules can make it less feasible or likely to sustain a late daytime focus), health (illness can dramatically change daytime productivity) and sleep patterns (light sleep linked to parenthood or being older can shift when you're most likely to be productive).

To discover your peak productivity, take a typical work day, divide it into one-hour slots and as you go through the day, look back at the previous hour and rate it on a scale of 0 (not focused, not productive) to 10 (very focused, very productive).

Do this for a few days and for one day on the weekend too if you have to work then on a task that requires your full focus. This will help you to determine whether or not the times you noted during the week linked to peak productivity are consistent on days you're not at work. If your peak work-day productivity is matched at the same time on the weekend, it means that your peak times are unrelated to the type of tasks you're completing and are instead linked to your high-performance times. Mary's peak productivity is between 7 and 9 a.m. and between 6 and 9 p.m. Once you spot your peak productivity, protect it and schedule your demanding work during those times you're more likely to sustain focus. This does not mean you're unlikely to focus at others times. What it means is that you're spotting the times your mind has strength of focus and using this knowledge to your advantage just like extraordinary people do.

Fuel your focus

The most simple step to support your focus is to make sure you've eaten! Protein is fuel for focus, so if you can turn to nuts, eggs, turkey, chicken – snacks or meals heavy on protein and light on carbohydrates – you'll fuel your focus for hours.

How Mary did it

Mary never knew when or if she would hear the 'all clear' from cancer. For one year whilst she had treatment, she had no idea if she had one month, one year, ten years or longer to live. Mary was clear on the cancer care programme she wished to develop with a team of like-minded people. She started working on it during her recovery. There were days she worked her *peak productivity times* and days she was unable to work. Mary *wiped out attention residue with the pressure of time* – she always had a target to achieve in the hour she knew she'd feel well after breakfast and before a chemotherapy session. Mary applied her learning about what led her cancer to grow unchecked and she extended *compassion* to herself, often picturing her children, who adored her, before focusing on some of the tough stuff, like writing her business plan, creating and securing a network of reliable like-minded men and women with equal passion to share care for others with cancer. Mary *supplemented her focus with Vitamin D* and she ate well. She committed to treating her body and mind well with *food to support recovery and focus.* Finally, Mary *planned, and she planned again* when plans did not work out because she was too sick and weak from chemotherapy. She readjusted her plans with smaller tasks for the times she was likely to feel ill, sometimes as small as, 'Send SMS to Allison about ordering the food cancer book.' For the times she was likely to feel well, she readjusted her plan to include more demanding tasks, such as, 'Write 1000 words for business plan.' Always there was the pressure of time since she had few hours without family responsibilities and without symptoms, pressure which science now demonstrates supports rather than diminishes focus.

How Can You Take This Forward?

In this chapter, we discovered the difference between helpful and unhelpful attention. We learned how to spot when we're self-focused simply by asking: Am I noticing the world around me? If the answer to this question is 'no' or if we're feeling self-conscious, a bit blue or unmotivated, chances are our attention has drifted inwards. Self-focused attention makes it hard to concentrate, gives us misleading information, and can make us feel like we're being stared at. It's also deeply unrewarding and will keep us stuck in an unproductive rut.

When your mind wanders, your attention has also become self-focused since mind-wandering takes you into your head rather than into the task at hand. Research on mind-wandering has led to different findings but the most consistent one is that it's unhelpful. So, unless you want to boost creativity to find new ways to use paperclips, it's best to notice when your focus has flown to the clouds and rein your attention back in.

Helpful attention is externally focused attention, where your focus is out of your head in the world or in the task at hand. Fortifying your focus to give your tasks your full attention will boost your mood, your productivity and will take you many steps forward on your path to extraordinary.

We covered thirteen steps to fortify your focus. First take the focus fitness test to assess your focus, then steps to strengthen it. Experiment with what works for you. If your focus consistently flies to your phone, you'll need to work hard to lengthen the times you can focus. But it's not impossible. The methods outlined in this chapter work. Get them working for you.

In a Nutshell

Unhelpful attention is focus that's gone inside ourselves to our thoughts, feelings and fears, or sensations in our body like our heart rate. It's also called *self-focused attention.*

Helpful attention is the kind of attention that's out of your head and in the world. It's called *externally focused attention* – attention we give to the task at hand, to other people and to what is going on moment to moment.

Self-focused attention is unhelpful
- It makes you feel self-conscious
- It makes it harder to concentrate
- It gives you misleading information
- It's unrewarding

Signs of self-focused attention are
- Feeling anxious, uncomfortable or self-conscious
- Being caught up in thoughts or questions that have no obvious answers
- Monitoring how you are coming across to other people
- Being over-aware of physical sensations, such as a racing heart or feeling shaky

A key question to spot if your attention has switched inwards is:
- Am I noticing the world around me?

Mind-wandering is mostly harmful. It's linked to
- Feeling blue
- Accelerated ageing
- The urge to give up

Mind-wandering about interesting topics can boost mood and, in specific conditions, creative problem-solving

It absolutely matters *what* you focus on and *how* you focus.

Tips to fortify your focus
- Welcome boring tasks
- Take the focus fitness test
- Train with the attention gym
- Clean up attention residue with the pressure of time
- Plan and plan again
- Check your Vitamin D
- Resist the temptation to give in when the going gets tough
- Change your attention filter
- Start out small and get bigger
- Work out what your go-to is and delay getting there
- Start the tough stuff with compassion
- Quit multi-tasking
- Spot your productivity peak
- Fuel your focus

IV.

Get Out of Your Head
With Helpful Thinking Habits

Anyone who has ever suffered nerves before giving a speech at an office party or a friend's wedding knows the instant relief that a glass of wine or a bottle of beer gives. Suddenly talking to 200 people feels manageable.

But the same speech without wine or beer beforehand feels terrifying.

Does alcohol make the speech go away and our terror with it? Or does it change what we focus on?

In one situation, our thoughts are focused on, What if I forget what I'm saying? What if I say something stupid or my mind goes blank?

In the other situation, we care a lot less about messing up. The alcohol relaxes our central nervous system and reduces our inhibitions. Because we expect it to relax our bodies, we allow our thinking to refocus. Instead of focusing on how tense we're feeling or what might go wrong, we refocus to what is actually going on.

My patients often ask why having a drink at the office party makes them feel more confident and I ask them: what is different about being at the party when you've had a drink compared to being there when you haven't had anything? How are your thoughts different?

In one situation, we're thinking, in the other we're observing. We change our focus from thinking about what might go wrong to observing what is going on. What we discover is that people are much less interested in us messing up than we are.

> Refocus your thinking from what might go wrong to observing what is actually going on.

I am certainly not advocating alcohol as a solution to anxiety. But what I am advocating is that we take control of our thinking so that we can enjoy feeling relaxed any time we choose, including in the stressed minutes leading up to a speech at the big office party.

This chapter introduces the key unhelpful thinking processes that will keep us stuck in a rut and shows how to kick them. Part of the training to think like a winner is to recognise the unhelpful habits and transform them. We need to develop healthy thinking habits too and we can do this at the same time. Healthy thinking, like happiness, can be trained. It's a skill we can learn.

1. Dwelling

Everyone does it. It's an unproductive pattern of thinking that becomes repetitive and, over time, addictive, just like smoking or drinking coffee or tea or turning to junk food when we're stressed. We tend to dwell more at night, when we're on our own, and when we're lost in unhappy thoughts. The more we do it, the more we strengthen the neural pathways in our brain, making it a default mode of thinking when we encounter disappointment or stress. Scientists now call it 'repetitive negative thinking' and it's one of the key processes that keep depression, traumatic stress and anxiety

GLL
Roehampton Library

Issue Summary

Patron: Miss ... a faria
Id: 0017*****
Date: 12/08/2010 05:34

Loaned today

Item: 90300000711825
Title: Be extraordinary : 7 key skills to
transform your life from ordinary to
extr
Due back: 23/06/2023 23:59

Current loans

Item: 90300000773376
Title: confident mind : a battle-tested
guide to unshakable performance
Due back: 17/06/202317/06/2023 23:59

Thank you for using self service

going. Kick this habit and there's an instant boost in our mood and productivity.

How can we spot it?

Dwelling is easily recognised by spotting our 'why', 'what if' and 'if only' thoughts. It's a circular thinking style that keeps us in a loop leading to no new information or answers or helpful behaviours.

'*What if* I hadn't said that?' '*What if* I had turned back and locked the door?' '*If only* I hadn't gone to the dentist that morning.' Or '*Why* did he say something so unkind?' '*Why* didn't I just say forget it?' '*Why* can't anything go right in my life?' '*Why* did the cancer come back?'

How does it affect us?

Since dwelling keeps us on a mental treadmill of repetitive negative thoughts, it stops us from thinking outside the box. This means that it blunts our creativity and our ability to problem-solve, which means we stay stuck in the problem rather than working our way out of it.

Imagine this:

You've arranged to cook a special dinner. It's a big family occasion. Your partner's family is travelling a long distance to eat with you. You're going to make a roast chicken. You have all the ingredients and plan to prepare the chicken first thing in the morning so it's ready for noon. When you get up, you sprinkle the chicken with herbs and oil. You switch the oven on then notice that it doesn't come on. You turn it off and on again. Again, you notice it doesn't come on.

In one scenario, you think, Why is the oven not working? Why did this have to happen today of all days? Why can't anything go right in my life? Why did it break down today? Why is it completely flat and dead but the other appliances are working? Why can't it just work on this one occasion? Why can't this one thing go right in my life?

How might you be feeling in this situation?

Now, imagine the same scenario again, but instead of thinking *Why* thoughts, you think, How can I get this chicken cooked by noon? How can I make this a great family get-together?

In the first scenario, we're more inclined to cancel our dinner. In the second, we're more inclined to find a solution, such as cooking the chicken at the neighbour's or preparing a meal on the stove top instead.

Unhappy feelings

Dwelling causes us to over-think and to feel unhappy. Usually we dwell on disappointments in our lives, situations where we may have felt unsure of ourselves or events we thought were difficult. But dwelling as a thinking style can become a habit, a loop we get stuck on when we think about everyday interactions and tasks.

Science shows that dwelling fuels depression and other unhappy states like anger, worry and anxiety. In one study, researchers asked people to give a speech under a lot of pressure and then got them to think in *whys* or *hows* after. They wanted to discover whether this kind of thinking was helpful or harmful after a difficult task, the kind of task that we might naturally dwell on in our own lives. To make the speech stressful, they told people in the study that how well they gave their speech was linked to how well they would succeed in their future careers. Since they needed everyone to have a similar negative experience to think about afterwards, they told everyone that they had failed the speech. The 'why' people were asked to think about why they had felt the way they had during the speech, and the 'how' group were asked to think about how they had felt moment by moment during the talk.

The scientists discovered that the people who had been asked to think in whys felt much bluer for the rest of the day compared to the people who had been asked to think in hows. They also had a lot more unwanted memories of the speech popping into their minds over the next week.

So not only does dwelling make us unhappy, it also makes unhappy memories pop into our minds more easily. It's the key thinking style that causes depression and keeps it going once in place. This makes sense given that once we start dwelling, we have more unhappy memories popping up, which keep us focused on unhappy thoughts, which understandably keeps us feeling blue. It's a vicious cycle, which leads to poor problem-solving, a deeper rut and more unhappy feelings.

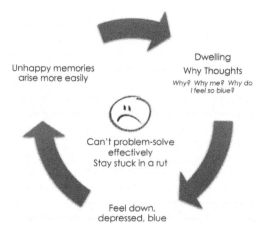

Unhappy memories
arise more easily

Dwelling
Why Thoughts
Why? Why me? Why do
I feel so blue?

Can't problem-solve
effectively
Stay stuck in a rut

Feel down,
depressed, blue

129

But dwelling also keeps post-traumatic stress going. Understandably, after a traumatic event like a car crash or a random act of violence, we would be inclined to think '*Why?*': '*Why* did this happen?', '*Why* me?' While this is normal in the aftermath of trauma, the more we focus on the *whys*, the more we keep our traumatic stress in place and the harder it gets to move on. It's important, as we'll see with Joyce below, to develop answers to our *why* thoughts and then take steps to think in *hows*.

New research also shows that an important time to avoid *why* thinking is during and right after a traumatic event like a car crash. My students and I ran a study where we showed people horrible films of real-life car crashes. We asked one group to think in *whys* while they were watching the film. '*Why* do events like this happen?' '*What if* this happened to me?' The other group focused on details such as exactly what was happening and how the car crash might be resolved. They focused on *how* thinking. We found that *why* thinking during the horrible films led to worse mood, more negative memories in the week after the film and many more traumatic stress symptoms one week later.

It's early days, but what it seems to suggest is that our thinking during and after a traumatic event can protect or harm us, and that thinking in *hows* is more helpful than thinking in *whys*.

Imagine this:

Four men go through the same minor annoyance but with different thoughts at the time. They all step in dog poo first thing on a Monday morning on their way to work.

The first man thinks: *Why* did I step in dog poo first thing on Monday morning? *Why* am I such a loser? *Why* do I do such stupid things?' He starts to feel low.

130

The second man walks out of his house and when his foot lands in dog poo, he thinks: *Why* did I step in dog poo? *Why* did I step in something that will contaminate my shoe? If I go back into the house, I'll contaminate my family. If I go to work, I will contaminate my colleagues. **If only** I had not done this! He feels worried, scared and anxious.

When the third man steps in dog poo, he thinks: *Why* did the stupid dog owner let his dog foul my doorstep? *Why* can't people be more considerate? *Why* do such idiots live on my street? This man feels angry.

When the fourth man walks out of his house and steps in dog poo, he thinks: Thank goodness I put my shoes on today! *How* can I get this off? He feels happy and relieved.

In this example we see that *why* thinking leads to unhappy feelings like anger, worry and sadness. *How* thinking is proactive and leads to happier feelings and more effective problem-solving.

How does this apply to everyday life?

The key message is to spot our '*why*' '*what if*' and '*if only*' thoughts and to recognise that when we have these thoughts, we are dwelling or ruminating and that there is no happy outcome with this kind of thinking. We then have to transform our *why* thinking to *how* thinking.

How can I change the situation in one small way now? How can I take one step to feel better now? How can I refocus my attention out of my head and into the task at hand? It's important to have a plan of action that we can turn to when we notice that we're dwelling. It will be different for all of us and we need to discover the most effective actions that will break the cycle.

Dealing with WHY THINKING

For events that we think could have gone better and we then replay over and over in our mind, such as a tough interview or an argument, we need to answer objectively the *why* question that runs through our mind, ask ourselves what we learned from the experience and swiftly move on to *how* thinking. We need to consider: Is there anything I could have done differently? Anything I could do in future to ensure a similar situation unfolds smoothly? Then we move on to *how* thinking.

This technique works wonders for patients I have treated who have suffered from post-traumatic stress disorder, who have often been plagued with *why* thoughts, such as: *Why* did the other driver drive so close to me?, *What if* I had decided to have the scan?, *Why* did I agree to allow my daughter to stay out late?

Together, like detectives on a mission, we uncover information from different sources, such as from the Internet, patients themselves, sometimes their relatives and other medical professionals, to come up informatively with answers to their troubling 'why' questions to the best of our ability, considering all the information that we now know and that patients have gathered since their trauma. We write out our detailed answers to their 'why' questions. When the *why* questions pop to mind, I encourage patients to read their written answers once only and move on to *how* thinking: *How* can I move forward? *How* can I feel better in this moment? I encourage them to remember that staying in the *why* frame of mind leads to no new information and makes the rut deeper.

Joyce's Story

In the 1950s, Joyce was a career woman, a junior doctor with the ambition to become a consultant. Her peers married and had children, halting their medical careers. Joyce did not marry, an unusual choice for a woman at the time. She excelled, saving lives in Saudi Arabia, Uganda, the United States and England. At the age of fifty-one, Joyce fell in love for the first time only to discover that her lover was struggling with his sexual orientation. Their relationship ended. Joyce then developed a rare form of blood cancer. She pulled through and was cancer-free for fifteen years. But it came back when she was sixty-eight. She was treated with a new drug in a medical study, the same drug as nine other people. Within five years, the nine other people had died. But Joyce, now seventy-five years old, recovered from her second bout of cancer. She then trained as a psychotherapist to counsel young men with schizophrenia.

What Joyce did

Joyce wrote answers, based on facts rather than feelings, to her *why* thoughts (Why did the cancer come back? Why me?). Then she focused on *how*. How can I feel better right now? How can I re-focus my attention to the task at hand?

How Joyce answered her why thoughts

Why did the cancer come back?

I developed myeloma, cancer of the blood, when I was fifty-one years old. I had chemotherapy to fight the cancer and took interleukin 2 to help my immune system. The five-year survival rate is only 40 per cent. The cancer went into remission and I was clear for 16 years. It is common for it to come back and it usually does return within five years in most people.

Why me ?

Myeloma can affect anyone. It doesn't help me to think about why I got it since there are no clear-cut answers. What I do know is that I am doing everything I can to be healthy and to do things I love doing while I still can. Seeing my nieces and nephews, travelling to Thailand and Bali, joining the choir in Richmond and touring England to sing. That's what's important to me.

Small steps

When Joyce spotted her *why* thoughts, she looked at her flashcards with her answers. Her repetitive thinking became a cue to get active. If it was early enough in the evening, she would walk in the park near her flat and notice the trees – their branches, their leaves – and other people. If it was late in the evening, she would sing. She would sing her favourite hymn.

What Joyce says

> 'It's impossible for me to feel down when I sing. It instantly gets me out of my head. I enjoy the sound, the words, the simplicity of the tune I am singing. I feel connected to the wider picture, to the beauty in life. That's what it's all about for me. Connection.'

The science: why does it work?

Getting active when we notice that we are dwelling gets us out of our heads and off the treadmill of negative thinking. It breaks the cycle and stops circular thinking, which means we stop fuelling low mood and further dwelling. It takes us out of our rut instead of deeper into it.

Singing, exercise, asking friends about what is new and good with them – all help to refocus our thoughts to what is actually going on in the here and now. Suddenly the *whys* and *what ifs* feel less important because we are giving them less attention and absorbing ourselves in an activity that needs our full attention.

When we're concentrating on strenuous cardiovascular exercise like a tough aerobics class or on singing a likeable tune, it's impossible to think about the *whys* and *what ifs*. That's because to sing or to exercise or to give a friend a helping hand, we need to focus on what we are doing and in so doing, our thoughts change from being focused on ourselves to being focused on the wider world and the people in it. We start to feel better. We begin weakening the neuronal pathways that reinforce *why* and *what if* thinking by choosing to respond differently to the familiar pull of *why, what if* and *if only*. We strengthen new pathways and new behaviours. Over time, like a muscle, we get stronger in choosing helpful responses when we notice the treadmill of negative thinking.

What to do when you notice you're dwelling

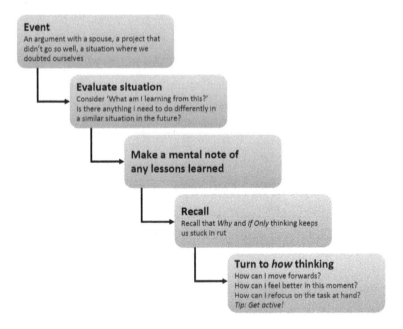

What not to do

Unless you are in the aftermath of a trauma or disappointment, do not call a friend and talk about the situation. This can keep you in a negative head space. While it is important to feel supported as we transition through upsetting events, continually talking about difficulties keeps us in the loop of circular thinking. Of course, it is helpful to chat to friends in the aftermath of trauma and disappointments, but we must be mindful also to focus on how to move forward when we seek support.

A note on loss and why thoughts

Loss of a job or a relationship is particularly disappointing and naturally gives rise to a lot of *why* thinking. Chapter VII, Cultivating

Happiness, presents Afet, who experienced severe loss following a medical misdiagnosis. Afet is an inspiring example of how to overcome *why* thinking linked to loss. Whilst answering *why* questions with facts can be helpful, it is also necessary to uncover the meaning of the loss we may be facing and what steps to take to introduce that meaning into our lives again. By doing this, we create the possibility of feeling a continuous connection to the positive meaning of what we have lost, whether that is a relationship, job or pet, for example. Chapter VII shows how to overcome the smaller losses in our everyday lives in step-by-step detail.

2. Catastrophising

If you have ever lost your mobile phone, you'll understand the gut-wrenching panic that hits the moment you realise it's gone. Some people will immediately jump to the worst possible outcomes and picture lost business and income, time and all their valuable contacts. Other people will momentarily panic, then remember the last time they backed it up, take steps to look for it or report it stolen and find a replacement.

Catastrophising is jumping to the worst possible conclusions. Usually when we catastrophise we also imagine in our mind's eye vivid pictures of our fears unfolding. As you will see in Chapter VI, Determination, research shows that 88 per cent of our worries do not come true. Yet, some of us will naturally be drawn to recall the rare occasions when our fears actually unfolded rather than the 88 per cent of occasions when everything worked out. Even when we do recall and rehearse the most negative outcome, we forget to recall that we also coped. This obviously keeps us feeling anxious.

Why do some people worry?

Worry is mostly a behaviour that we learn. We are more likely to have learned to worry if one or both of our parents were worriers. But we also unintentionally teach ourselves to worry and so worrying, as a behaviour, can get strengthened over time. For example, if we have a speech to give and start worrying about how it will unfold and it then unfolds without hiccups, we learn that worrying beforehand was helpful. That's because our brain links our experience of the speech going well with behaviours beforehand, one of them being worry. We can end up learning all sorts of unhelpful links. In this example, we learn that worrying leads to better speeches and so some of us will be more likely to worry when asked to give another one. Other people will learn that because the presentation went well, there's less need to worry in the future and their worrying will decrease over time. Genes also play a role in determining who is likely to worry excessively. The one that has attracted the most attention is the serotonin transporter gene.

The serotonin transporter gene

Serotonin is a chemical found in our bodies, mostly in our digestive tracts but also in our blood and central nervous system, and has a key role in helping us to feel happy. The serotonin transporter gene recycles serotonin after it is released into the synapse between neurons in our brain. It pulls serotonin back in from the space between neurons for reuse. How much serotonin is pulled back in and reused depends on the length of the gene's promoter region, the part of the gene that controls how much serotonin transporter is made and how often.

There are two versions of this gene: a short and a long version. We inherit two copies of each gene, one from each parent, and many of us will have inherited two copies of the long version of the gene. Some people will have inherited one long and one short copy of the gene, and some people will carry two copies of the short version of the gene.

The effect

Having the short copies of the gene is linked to depression and anxiety. After Hurricane Katrina, for example, scientists discovered that people who had one copy of the short version or two copies of the short version were twice as likely to get PTSD compared to people who had inherited two copies of the long version of the gene.

The promoter region is shorter in people with short copies of the gene, meaning that their serotonin synthesis may be less adaptive compared to people with long copies of the gene. Long copies of the gene produce more protein product, which can grab more serotonin from the synapse. Cells with long copies of the gene take up twice as much serotonin from the synapse as cells with one or two short copies of the gene. So, people who have inherited two long copies of the serotonin transporter gene may be recycling more serotonin than people with short copies of the gene.

Scientists have also discovered that people who have one or two copies of the short version of the serotonin transporter gene have a smaller amygdala, the part of the brain also known as the fear centre. When something potentially scary, like a snake, presents itself, the amygdala reacts, sending signals to another part of the limbic system called the cingulate, a key brain region linked to emotion, learning and memory. A signal travels within the cingulate, which then slows down or revs up the activity of the amygdala. People with two long copies of the serotonin transporter gene are naturally better able to damp down the amygdala when it becomes active to potential threat if needed. So, they might see the snake and then realise that it's a garden snake, which is metres away and therefore not a threat.

For people with just one short copy of the gene, the signal to and from the amygdala into the cingulate is weaker. So, their amygdala gets revved up instead of damping down. They might see the snake and think it's lethal and an immediate threat. They'll instantly feel anxious and brace themselves for a fight.

It's all about connection or connectivity

The serotonin transporter gene affects the connection between the amygdala and the cingulate. When this is not very strong, as in people with a short copy of the serotonin transporter gene, then the amygdala is more active and responsive to potential fear. People with long copies of the gene have better communication between their amygdala and cingulate, so naturally respond with less anxiety to possible fearful things.

The good news

Changing our **THINKING** truly does change our **BRAIN**

Genes are only a small part of how we respond to stress. A field of science called epigenetics is uncovering how the environment can change our DNA and the function of our genes, but not their structure. So, our genes, our biology, need not be destiny. We can influence the function of our genes by changing our environment and this includes changing our thinking. A lot of research shows that the way we think affects serotonin and vice versa. One group of investigators found that when people recalled happy memories this boosted their serotonin synthesis compared to when they recalled sad memories. A new area of research is looking at how cognitive behavioural therapy (CBT) changes our brain. A team in the US found that there is better connection or connectivity between brain regions after a course of CBT for depression.

Are there ways to increase serotonin?

Exercise

Exercise increases serotonin, our feel-good chemical. Moving about and getting our hearts beating quickly in aerobic exercise increases the firing rate of serotonin neurons and releases more tryptophan in the brain, which is the precursor to serotonin. So, exercise leads to more serotonin, but it must be exercise that really gets our hearts pumping.

Light

Our ancestors worked outdoors in fields and so were exposed to much more light and vigorous exercise than we are, so they may have had more serotonin and happier moods than we do today. We synthesise more serotonin on days when there is more sunlight. Light maintains levels of tryptophan, the precursor to serotonin. But it has to be bright light, such as outdoor light or a special lamp that is about six times brighter than a household kitchen light.

Thoughts

Changing our thoughts can rewire our brains. In a classic study looking at the effect of CBT on the brains of people with a fear of spiders, scientists discovered that CBT changed patterns of activation in the brain linked to fear. After CBT, when looking at pictures of spiders, people who had been scared of spiders had the same brain activation as people who were never scared of spiders. Another study showed that people who recovered from depression with CBT had less metabolism in the part of their brain involved in thinking and planning (prefrontal cortex) and better connectivity in the emotion centres (cortical-limbic areas).

Tryptophan

Tryptophan is an amino acid, found in protein like turkey, that gets converted to serotonin in the brain. But only purified tryptophan, found in supplements, can increase serotonin in our brains. It was once thought that eating tryptophan-rich foods like turkey would boost serotonin in the brain. It does not. That's because tryptophan competes with other amino acids to get into the brain after a meal rich in protein, and the rise in our blood of the other amino acids prevents the rise in tryptophan from being transported to the brain.

Back to catastrophising

The way to tackle catastrophising is to recognise when we are doing it and to take a moment to think about any advantages it offers. Usually there are none. What are the disadvantages? Typically, catastrophising makes us feel worse, lowers our mood and makes it hard to problem-solve. As we have just seen, this type of anxious thinking activates the amygdala and heightens our fearful feelings.

The key to transforming this type of thinking is to recognise that we are jumping to conclusions, to remind ourselves that most of our worries have a good outcome and that we can cope. We can cope with whatever comes our way.

Replace your pictures

Learn to replace fearful images with positive ones. For example, stop yourself from imagining you'll mess up your speech and picture instead a happy, calm, confident image of you enjoying your speech. Images have a much more immediate effect on our

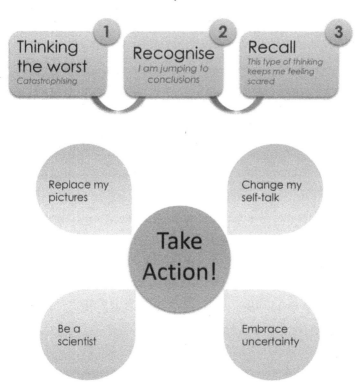

mood than thoughts alone so practise conjuring up positive images of performing well. In one study (also covered in Chapter I), scientists asked people to talk to a stranger twice while holding a positive or negative image of themselves in mind. The researchers told some of the participants to hold a negative image in mind first and then a positive one in the second conversation. They told other participants to hold a positive image in mind first and then a negative one in their second conversation. They discovered something fascinating: whenever people pictured a negative image of themselves, whether it was in the first or second speech, they always performed worse and felt more anxious. Our images affect our feelings and our performance. Keep them positive!

Change your self-talk

Stop telling yourself that it will turn out badly and change this to, 'I'll cope with whatever happens. It will work out.' These types of thoughts immediately reduce your anxiety and with less anxiety, you'll problem-solve more effectively.

Be a scientist: turn it into an experiment

Take the catastrophe you're worried about and turn it into an experiment instead of rehearsing it in your mind. Be curious about it. Note what you are worried will happen, write it down, and put your experiment away until you are ready to note the outcome, what actually happened. This table will help you.

Here is one of Joyce's experiments.

Situation	Predictions	Experiment	Outcome	What I learned
Going to see doctor.	They'll tell me my test results are worse. I'll crumble and I won't be able to ask my questions.	Meet with the doctor. Take my list of questions. Tell them I would like to ask questions. Then go through them one by one.	My test results showed some concern in that there hasn't been much improvement, but there hasn't been any deterioration either. I feel sad and also relieved.	My predictions weren't correct. They were based on how scared I was feeling beforehand and the images I had of ill health. I coped. I took care of myself, took time to ask my questions. This helped me to feel calmer and to plan some steps with my doctor for the future.

Embrace uncertainty

For many people, fear of uncertainty increases anxiety. Our life-styles demand certainty and we plan so that we are prepared for unexpected events before they arise, such as a change in weather, delays in transport or minor illnesses. But there are some big life events we can't plan for: falling in love, developing a serious illness or experiencing a sudden trauma. While there are unexpected difficult events that cross our paths, unexpected good events happen with the same frequency. Joyce's recovery from cancer is one example. Knowing that we can cope, that we will take reasonable steps to manage catastrophe if it does strike, will help to weaken our fear of uncertainty. Keeping our attention focused in the here and now will do this too as will taking control of our thoughts so they don't trail off to picture feared scenarios.

3. Black-and-white Thinking

Thinking in polarised ways about problems can keep people stuck in a rut. 'It will never work out' or 'The train is always late' are examples of thinking in extremes. Cognitive behavioural thinking encourages us to think in shades of colour. This kind of thinking is linked to happier moods. 'I've done everything I can to help in this situation. It may work out, but if it doesn't I know I have done the best I can' and 'Sometimes the train is late, but mostly it's on time'. In cognitive behavioural language we call these alternative thoughts.

Perhaps the most extreme example of black-and-white thinking are prejudices, such as 'Californians are flaky' or 'All women are out to snare a millionaire'.

What one psychologist, Christine Padesky, has shown in the United States is that the thoughts that drive depression and low self-esteem are a lot like a prejudice. Beliefs like 'I'm worthless', 'I'm a failure', 'I'm useless', which keep depression in place, operate like a prejudice.

What are the qualities of prejudices?

We saw in Chapter I, Vision, that people with strong black-and-white beliefs discount information that fails to support their strong negative belief. It's like thinking 'Californians are flaky' then when we meet someone from California who is articulate and successful, instead of modifying our beliefs about Californians, we discount the information. We say, 'This Californian is an exception to the rule' and we go on believing that Californians are flaky.

Holding strong negative beliefs about ourselves drives us to discount positive information, like a compliment, that fails to fit with our beliefs rather than modifying or updating our negative belief with this new information.

People who thrive update their beliefs. They think in shades of colour rather than in black and white. They look at the world with a flexible filter that updates their thoughts when they become outdated, inaccurate and unhelpful.

The following are examples of extreme thoughts linked to moments when we may be feeling low in self-esteem and examples of how one might update them with flexible thinking. You will see that the format for updating thoughts is to first make the distinction between feelings and your interpretations of feelings. You may feel inadequate from time to time, but this does not mean you are inadequate. Uncomfortable feelings are not evidence that a negative belief about yourself is true. The next step would be to go out of your way to note evidence that fails to fit with the extreme thought. Then, think about the best meaning of the evidence: what does it say about you as a person? This will lead to a flexible, updated thought.

Extreme Thoughts	Updated Thoughts
I am inadequate	I may feel inadequate because my boss passed me over for a promotion, but this does not mean I am inadequate. My manager gave positive and constructive feedback in my performance review that I'll take forward. What this means is that I am a competent and proactive person who, at times, can feel inadequate in response to disappointments.
I am unlikeable	I may feel unlikeable but this does not mean I am unlikeable. I have been invited to parties and days out with friends. My colleagues have made tea for me and chatted in the coffee room. What this means is that I am a likeable person who, at times, feels unlikeable.
I am vulnerable	I feel vulnerable when I feel low or when my ex-partner calls to argue. When I am immersed in my yoga class, I feel strength and calm. I ended a long-term relationship that wasn't working. What this means is that I am strong individual who understandably feels vulnerable from time to time.

Flexible thinking is more likely than extreme thinking to lead to proactive behaviours, such as applying for the next promotion, reaching out to friends or exercising, all of which can improve mood and self-esteem.

What Joyce did

When Joyce was fifty-one years old, she fell in love for the first time only to discover that Frank, the man of her dreams, was gay. Joyce used to replay in her mind the painful moment when he told her that he was finally certain that he was gay and wouldn't be able to have a romantic relationship with her. Joyce felt rejected, ashamed and devastated, particularly when she thought about that moment. She asked herself what it meant to her that he rejected her. Joyce believed that it meant that she was unattractive, different and unlovable.

Joyce recognised that this was painful black-and-white thinking that kept her feeling low. So she changed the lens through which she was seeing the world. That Frank chose to have a relationship with a man was not a reflection of how attractive or lovable Joyce was. Thinking about it like this helped Joyce to feel more empowered and she changed her thoughts to: I feel attractive when I wear my favourite dresses. My personality is attractive – fun and upbeat. My experience of being rejected in a relationship makes me more similar than different to other people, and I know that I am lovable. I feel this especially around my nieces and nephews.

Flexible thinking led Joyce to choose active behaviours, such as visiting her nieces and friends, rather than withdrawing from them. This supported her belief of being lovable, which led to more active behaviours and extraordinary success. Joyce's success included developing rich and meaningful friendships, more loving relationships with her nieces and nephews, daily moments of joyfulness, and what she described as a warmer connection to people and the activities she loved. She recovered from her second bout of cancer, retrained as a psychotherapist and helped to transform the lives of young men suffering from the devastating psychological disorder, schizophrenia.

4. Emotional Reasoning and Over-generalising

Emotional reasoning is dangerous! We fall into emotional reasoning when we prioritise our feelings and assume they reflect reality. For example, when we feel nervous and anxious, we often think we look this way to other people. We believe that because we feel nervous we must look nervous, because we feel guilty we must be guilty, because we feel that something bad might happen, then something bad will happen.

After a traumatic event, my patients feel as though they are more at risk of enduring another one because they understandably feel scared. But their risk of suffering trauma does not increase with every unexpected catastrophe. How scared they feel because they have been through something frightening is not a sign that something bad is about to happen. It's a sign of emotional reasoning. Usually when people go through a traumatic event, their sense of danger expands or, in CBT language, their sense of danger over-generalises. Because they feel scared, they overestimate the likelihood of something bad happening. This affects their behaviour, so instead of observing what is going on when they are out and about, they understandably focus on signs of danger, which keep fearful thoughts and feelings in place.

Even in the absence of a traumatic event, we often fall into emotional reasoning. For example, we may believe that because we feel nervous and uncomfortable, we look this way to other people. We use our feelings to make judgements about how we come across to other people rather than making judgements based on their feedback. Research shows that when people watch themselves on a video recording and pretend that, instead of seeing themselves, they are watching an actor or a stranger on television, they are much better at viewing themselves objectively. Their judgements of their performance are then much more similar to how other people judge them. Feelings are an unreliable source of information about how we come across to other people, and we must learn to form judgements about ourselves based on objective indicators like feedback from colleagues and friends.

Patients I have treated and the extraordinary people I have interviewed who thrive and who continue to thrive after adversity do not identify with their emotions. Emotions are feelings that we experience but they are not who we are. Like thoughts they come and go, and it is best to experience them in this way. People who thrive after trauma recognise that their traumatic event is an event in the past and does not increase their risk of experiencing an unpleasant event in the future. They make judgements about risk based on fact rather than feeling. They do not equate fear with probability.

People who thrive recognise that their sad feelings will pass and use their emotions as a cue to get active so they may transform a feeling state they no longer wish to prolong. As soon as we feel angry, sad, scared or disappointed, it's a cue to stop thinking, focus our attention on what is happening now, focus on facts not feelings, then get active, taking steps to make ourselves feel better.

Extraordinary

Proactive
Solution-focused **Thinking**

Active
Responsible language

5. Extraordinary Thinking

Proactive

Extraordinary thinking is proactive. It's about how. People transitioning from ordinary to extraordinary think big. They think long-term about what they want to achieve. If they've been through a medical misdiagnosis, their future story does not stop at the worst moment. It goes beyond recovery. It includes what they can do to make sure medical mistakes don't happen again. They might consider what tools need to be developed so hospitals improve. They may consider how they can go about helping to develop those tools.

Active

Extraordinary thinking is linked to active behaviours. These people pick up the telephone, they get active in spite of feeling insecure, tired, scared and overwhelmed with what they've been through. They know that by getting active, they stop their negative unhelpful thinking and it moves them one step closer to their goals. These people know they have nothing to lose and that the worst thing about trying is that it may feel uncomfortable. The best thing is that it moves them towards their goals and it helps them to feel more upbeat.

Solution-focused

People who continue to thrive after setbacks look for solutions. They turn *why* thinking to *how* thinking. They take risks. When doctors tell them they won't walk again, they make it their mission to walk again. They find out what they need to do, what devices they will need to help support their mobility. They see problems as challenges and they rise even though they may feel scared, let down and hurt.

Responsible language

Importantly, people who thrive take responsibility for how they feel. They do not blame others even when other people are clearly at fault. They recognise that they control their feelings and they have a choice.

Taking responsibility for our feelings involves responsible language, or what CBT calls 'reframing'. For example, we might think: 'My mother makes me feel frustrated' or 'I am upset my boss did not select me for promotion'.

Responsible language transforms these thoughts to: 'I feel frustrated around my mother' and 'When I think about my boss's decision, I upset myself'.

By making ourselves the active agent, the steps to feel better become more apparent. Knowing that we may feel frustrated around certain people helps us to take care of ourselves so that we put active steps in place to feel less frustrated in these situations, such as by limiting contact, by steering away from certain topics or by saying how we feel.

In terms of unpleasant events, such as missing out on a promotion, we recognise that if thinking about it is upsetting, then we need to change the way we think about it. We need to consider key questions:

- What is it about the event that is upsetting?
- What does it say about me as a person?
- How can I update the meaning?
- What behaviours will support my updated thoughts?

How Joyce updated thoughts linked to rejection

You'll recall that when the love of Joyce's life rejected her, she believed it meant that she was unattractive, different and unlovable. Joyce took responsibility for how she felt and considered whether or not how she was interpreting the rejection was accurate. She realised that Frank's sexual orientation was not an indication of how lovable or attractive she was. Then she updated her thoughts. You may recall that she chose to think: I feel attractive when I wear my favourite dresses. My personality is attractive – fun and upbeat. My experience of being rejected in a relationship makes me more similar than different to other people, and I know that I am lovable. I feel this especially around my nieces and nephews.

Interpret ambiguity in positive ways

A positive bias helps people to thrive. That's a tendency to interpret ambiguous information positively rather than negatively. For example, people with a positive bias are likely to interpret a stranger smiling as a sign that this person is being friendly rather than mocking them. If they see a friend on the street who ignores them, they're more likely to think their friend didn't see them rather than that they were ignoring them.

In cognitive behavioural terms, this is called a *positive interpretation bias*. There is an enormous amount of research that shows that a bias towards interpreting ambiguous cues in a threatening or negative way is linked to anxiety and traumatic stress.

The good news is there is also a lot of research to show that we can train ourselves to interpret ambiguity positively and that the effects last. Training involves reading ambiguous scenarios and being given the positive interpretation. This creates a positive interpretation bias and this effect extends into our everyday life, raising our mood and leading us to interpret ambiguous scenarios positively.

You can practise below and there is more in-depth training on the www.beextraordinarybook.com website.

The Thinking Gym

thinking gym

The correct answers are in bold. Circle them!

People laugh after something you said. They think you are **funny** / embarrassing.

A friend does not respond when you wave hello. They are **distracted** / mad.

153

Your boss wants to meet with you. She will criticise / **praise** you.

An old friend comments on how you look different now. He thinks you are ugly / **attractive**.

Dealing with indecision

People who transition from ordinary to extraordinary make decisions and limit the time they're in limbo. They recognise that there are an infinite number of possibilities they can explore to be happy and that the decision they face, unless it's one of life or death, offers different paths that will lead to more possibilities to explore to be happy. They do not get stuck with indecision. They make a decision and over time they make it the right decision.

How Can You Take This Forward?

The unhelpful thinking styles that keep us stuck in a rut are dwelling, catastrophising, black-and-white thinking, over-generalisation and emotional reasoning. The techniques described in this chapter show how to overcome these thinking styles. Which processes are holding you back? Refer back to the relevant sections in this chapter to review steps to overcome them. 'In a Nutshell' summarises key points to put into practice today so you can start to kick the unhelpful processes and practise helpful habits to move forward on the path to extraordinary.

In a Nutshell

Helpful thinking involves getting out of your head and getting active. This also gets you out of your painful emotion.

You are not emotion. They come and go and intensify with unhelpful thinking and become manageable with helpful thinking styles.

Transform *why* thinking to *how* thinking.

Make a list of what you can do when you notice you are dwelling and thinking in *whys*. Use the flow chart in this chapter to help.

Recognise that catastrophising is the trap of jumping to conclusions. Don't fall in. Remember 88 per cent of worries have a good outcome.

Be a scientist: turn your fear into an experiment.

Use positive imagery to boost your mood and picture the most likely outcome.

Increase serotonin. Exercise. Get outdoors. Think in shades of colour.

Avoid identifying with your most painful emotion. Realise it will pass.

Be active, be proactive, be solution-focused.

Take responsibility for your feelings. It guides you to be active.

Learn to interpret ambiguity positively to support helpful beliefs about yourself.

Make decisions, don't dilly-dally. Recognise that each choice leads to different opportunities to explore to be happy and that, over time, you can make your decision the right decision. Don't delay deciding.

V.

Extraordinary Behaviours

The clocks have gone back, it's pitch black when your feet hit the pavement after work and you know you should head to the gym. You tell yourself you should work out and the more you say this, the more you absolutely want to avoid it.

Does this sound familiar? You know you should do something, and your mind offers many reasons to avoid what you know you should do.

Whether you are putting off work needed for a deadline or avoiding exercise, avoidance is the number-one behaviour that will keep you stuck in a rut. It is also the number-one behaviour that keeps anxiety and depression going. Achieving an extraordinary life means kicking avoidance and choosing what is best for you rather than what is easiest.

Easier said than done, though, right? In this chapter, we'll discover what avoidance is a sign of, how to spot your triggers to avoid, and what to do with them. We'll learn from Caroline, a young woman who quit heroin by herself while raising her daughter. Years after she had pushed heroin into her past, she was brutally attacked; she recovered and went on to study nursing before moving to Cambodia to pioneer a health centre for sick and bereaved children.

Nothing requires stronger commitment to choosing new behaviours than overcoming drug addiction. What can Caroline teach us about overcoming triggers to stuck-in-the-rut behaviours?

In my work with hundreds of patients, it has become clear that there are nine steadfast ways to overcome avoidance and four key behaviours to keep you on your extraordinary track. This chapter will show you what they are, the science behind them and how to incorporate them into your life.

Caroline's Story

Caroline came from a regular, middle-class family in France. She took a detour in her teens and got hooked on heroin. Turning to prostitution to pay for her habit, she ended up having a baby with her dealer. This wake-up call motivated her to get off heroin. She separated from her dealer and moved to the UK with her daughter. Several years later, when she was thirty-five years old, a convicted rapist was released from prison on parole. He pretended to be a police officer and entered her flat, brutally assaulting her in front of her then six-year-old daughter. Today Caroline is a well-respected nurse pioneering new healthcare systems in villages in Cambodia.

1. Get Ahead of 'Should' Thinking

The moment we tell ourselves we 'should' do something is the moment we summon a desire to avoid doing it. It is one of the uncanny phenomena linked to thinking. The more we tell ourselves we must do something, the harder it becomes to do. The more we tell ourselves not to do something, the more we want to do it. We see it most clearly in post-traumatic stress disorder. The more patients tell themselves not to think about their trauma, the more it pops into their minds. The harder they try to push their frightening memories away, the more frequently they reappear.

Try this:

> For the next twenty seconds, I give you permission to think about anything you want, anything at all.
>
> The one thing I don't want you to think about is *the fluffy bunny rabbit* with floppy ears and the red bow tie smiling at you.
>
> Go on, think about anything at all. Anything.
>
> But you should not think about the bunny rabbit with floppy ears and his red bow tie. Try hard not to think about this curious, cute *bunny rabbit.*
>
> Do not think of the *bunny rabbit* and his bow tie!

What do you notice?

Most people find that as soon as they tell themselves to stop thinking about something, the thought or picture of it immediately springs back to mind like a tightly wound toy.

Fyodor Dostoevsky, the Russian author most famous for his works *Crime and Punishment* and *The Idiot*, first noted this phenomenon in 1863 in his travel accounts of Western Europe when he wrote: *Try to pose for yourself this task: not to think of a polar bear, and you will see that the cursed thing will come to mind every minute.*

A century later, psychologist Daniel Wegner at Harvard University investigated the phenomenon. He devised a simple experiment where he told students to try not to think of a white bear and to press a bell if they did while they talked through their thoughts for five minutes. His team found that even though the students had been given clear instructions to avoid thinking of a white bear, thoughts of the bear popped into their minds at least once per minute. The team then switched tack, asking the same students to try hard to think about a white bear, rather than suppress it, for the next five minutes. Interestingly, first trying hard to avoid thinking of the bear and then trying hard to think of the bear caused even more thoughts of white bears to come to mind compared to students who had been given permission right from the beginning to think of white bears. This clever study showed that suppressing thoughts causes them to rebound later. So began an exciting new field of research to understand why telling yourself to stop thinking about something makes you think about it even more.

Over the course of his career, Wegner developed a theory to explain why it's tough to push away unwanted thoughts, which he called *ironic processes theory*. He carried out a series of studies, demonstrating that when people try hard to avoid thinking of something, one part of the mind does avoid the thought whilst another part checks to make sure the thought is not there, which, of course, ironically brings it to mind. This is why telling yourself you 'should not' think of a particular thought or topic makes it come to mind more often.

When it comes to behaviour, the more you tell yourself you 'should' do something, the more you strengthen the desire for the opposite: of not doing that thing. This is because the people who have most often used 'shoulds' in our lives and from a young age are stern parents or teachers. Their expectations and rules restricted our desires at one time or another, leading some of us to rebel and others to dream of doing so.

160

When our thoughts include 'should', we may hear the voice of a critical parent or teacher in our mind. We may even experience a feeling similar to the past when we were told off but without the memory for the event coming to mind. Psychologists call it *affect without recollection*, when you feel an emotion linked to a past event without remembering the event at the same time. So, you hear 'should' in your mind and you instantly feel disgruntled.

Chances are you have internalised the voice that belongs to the past person who nagged you with lots of 'shoulds': you should exercise, do your homework, clean your room, reply to that email, wash the dishes, write your thank-you cards, pay your telephone bill, and so on. Psychologists call this the *internalised critic or parent*. We are naturally primed to rebel like disgruntled teenagers when we hear the word 'should' no matter how logical or healthy the suggestion is.

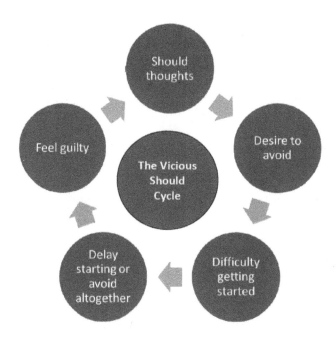

'Should' thinking makes it hard to get started and usually ends up with us feeling badly about ourselves. When we feel badly about ourselves, we're more likely to make bad or unhealthy decisions – like staying put on the couch, skipping the gym or delaying working on a deadline. Overcoming avoidance means nipping 'should' thinking in the bud by learning to use *future-feeling thinking*.

Decision-making – a common mistake

Most people make decisions based on how they are feeling in the moment rather than on how they want to feel. So, one of the key ways to kick avoidance is to consider how you want to feel in the future and to be guided by this today. Make decisions with *future-feeling thinking*. If going to the gym will make you feel energised and happy, make your decision to go based on how it will make you feel rather than on how tired or flat you may be feeling beforehand.

My patients often tell me, 'I know I should exercise. I know I will feel better afterwards but I really do not feel like it' and because they do not feel like it, they struggle to follow through with trying a new behaviour. 'I know I should call my friend, but I do not feel like it.'

I teach my patients how to use *future-feeling thinking* to overcome their 'should' thinking.

Future-feeling thinking

When you notice a 'should' thought come to mind, replace it with a question about how you will feel in the future. 'How will I feel after I have been to the gym?' or 'How will I feel when I can tick that phone call off my to-do list?'

Thinking about how we will feel after we have worked out or ticked off an unexciting task on our to-do list is the feeling we are seeking to guide our decisions to act today. 'How will I feel after I have been to the gym?' is likely to lead to 'I will feel energised and enjoy a sense of achievement.' 'How will I feel when I can tick that phone call off my to-do list?' is likely to lead to 'I will feel relief and a sense of achievement.'

Relief and a sense of achievement are far more rewarding and motivating than the consequences of staying put, avoiding the gym or avoiding the phone call.

My clients feel uplifted when they try something new. I encourage them to use the memory of feeling energised as motivation to try their new behaviour again. The more they try their new behaviours, the more evidence they gather that links their new behaviour with feeling upbeat. The stronger the association becomes between 'new behaviour' and 'feeling good', the harder it becomes to avoid.

Trying a new behaviour just once is all that is needed to plant the seed of a new habit. The more we try our new behaviour and feel upbeat, the more we strengthen the neural circuitry to support our new habit.

I just need to try it once?

Trying your new behaviour once is a good start. But science tells us that it can take anywhere from 18 to 264 days to build a new habit. The good news is that you don't need to try the new behaviour every day. But you do need to try it.

To discover how habits take root in everyday life, Phillippa Lally at University College London asked people to choose a new behaviour linked to eating, drinking or another activity and to try it every day for twelve weeks. Unsurprisingly they found that the more a behaviour is repeated the more automatic it becomes. But people really differed in how quickly their habit became automatic. Some people needed just eighteen days and others needed three-quarters of a year. The type of behaviour, the person and the circumstances all affected how quickly the habit became automatic. It was much faster for a habit like drinking more water to become automatic than jogging every day for fifteen minutes. Reassuringly, it really didn't make a difference if people missed practising their new habit once, but they had to practise the habit most days to make it automatic. What this means is that there's not a lot of wiggle room when you're making new habits stick so think carefully about what habit you want to nurture then address the obstacles that could stop you from trying it.

Most people say when they start exercise or other behaviour they've been putting off, that they're happy they started and once they got going, it was easy to keep going. It's much like jumping into a freezing pool. It's hard to do, but once you're in there, you're glad you dove right in.

2. How to Cross the Start Line

The three-minute carrot

If you are struggling to get started, give yourself permission to try the new behaviour for just three minutes, then reassess how you are feeling,

> The key to overcoming avoidance is learning how to cross the start line rather than striving to reach the finish line.

giving yourself permission to carry on for another three minutes if you choose to or to stop.

What this does is create a guilt-free get-out clause and presents you with something manageable to try. Rather than 'I should run for fifteen minutes' you change this to 'I am going to run for three minutes and at three minutes, I'll review how it's going and stop if I want to. Anybody can run for three minutes, including me.' At three minutes you stop, praise yourself, then offer yourself the opportunity to run for another three minutes, with the permission to stop if you want to. What you are doing is building up a series of achievable steps that motivate the next step and before you know it, you have run for fifteen minutes or you have made it easier to run for six minutes the next day. What an awesome sense of achievement you'll feel!

Allow yourself to do an average job rather than a perfect job

This is exactly how one of my clients learned to floss her teeth every day. She told herself to try it once and gave herself permission to do a bad job, to miss teeth and to do it quickly but at least to floss. The next day she gave herself permission to try it again and also to do a poor job. After three weeks of flossing and missing out teeth, she gave herself permission to try it properly once. Trying it properly was easy because she had already made a change in her routine from not flossing to doing some flossing. Starting to floss properly after days of doing an okay job was manageable and something she has been able to carry on with for years.

> **Allow yourself to do an average job rather than a perfect job.**

Schedule your new behaviour with a friend

It is much harder to avoid the gym or other new behaviour if you have committed to someone else and they are waiting for you.

Schedule a reward for once you've achieved your new behaviour

A common technique, called the Pomodoro Technique, is to work for twenty-five minutes and break for five minutes. During the twenty-five minutes you focus your attention on the task at hand, knowing you will enjoy a reward for five minutes afterwards. Choose rewards that give you a complete break like getting up from your desk to feed the birds or stroke your pets. After four chunks of twenty-five minutes and linked five-minute breaks, give yourself a longer break for twenty minutes or so.

List why the new behaviour is important to you

List the reasons why the new behaviour is important to you, why you thought about starting it in the first place. Email the list to your phone and look at it in your times of wavering willpower.

Picture success

Create an image of success in your mind's eye of you achieving your new behaviour days before you plan to start it. Use all of your senses. For example, if your new behaviour is to run at the gym every Monday and Wednesday, first picture yourself leaving work on Monday and what you will be feeling. Will you have any doubts about going to the gym? Picture yourself overcoming your wavering willpower, reminding yourself that you are choosing to run to improve your health, so you have more energy with your kids . . .

or whatever the reason is. Then picture yourself in your gym kit sweating on the treadmill. Consider how your whole body will feel. How will your legs and feet feel? Will you be holding the handrails on the treadmill or moving your arms freely? Will you be breathless? Where will you feel sweat on your body? Will you feel it running down your face? Will your gym have a particular smell? Call it to mind in your image. See yourself achieve 15 minutes of running. Picture yourself afterwards, sipping from your water bottle and heading to the changing room. How will you feel? Bring the feeling into your image. When your mind offers an excuse to give in, call to mind the elated image of you having finished your run with sweat trickling down your face, the taste of water quenching your thirst and your immense satisfaction and pride in performing well.

Imagery is one of the more powerful tools to support you in preparing for success. In Chapter I, Vision, we saw that elite athletes are trained to use imagery to prime their minds and bodies to succeed. Vivid imagery triggers neural firings to muscles and can prepare you mentally for challenges. For an athlete, a challenge may be how to deliver a winning serve. For us, it is likely to be how to respond to wavering willpower. Imagine yourself responding to the urge to give in with a picture of you succeeding. The key is to create your image days before you plan to start your new behaviour and to visualise the image in detail in real time. This means if it takes five minutes to leave the office and those are the five minutes when your willpower is most likely to wane, then spend five minutes visualising leaving work and seeing yourself overcome your wavering willpower. Trained Navy Seal officer and athlete Nick Norris uses imagery to overcome hesitation and doubt that he could face when bouldering at a great height. He practises rock climbing manoeuvres over and over in his mind's eye to perfect his performance. In Chapter I, we learned how Jessica Ennis, Novak Djokovic, and Wayne Rooney use imagery to succeed. Boxer Muhammad Ali also constantly pictured winning his matches. All of these athletes crossed the start line and achieved extraordinary success.

Take a selfie

Along the same lines of seeing success in your imagery, actually take a photo of your success. For example, when you run at the gym, take a selfie on your phone. A photo is a tangible reminder of your achievement, what you can experience if you follow through with your new behaviour, and will motivate you to try the behaviour again. It is difficult to respond to a photo of success with a decision to avoid the behaviour linked to success. Your photo of you, benefiting from the health positives of exercise, for example, will help you over the hurdle of taking no action.

Enlist the help of a behaviour buddy

Describe your goal to a friend, explaining why the behaviour is important to you and that you are going to need their support. Figure out what you need from your friend to support you through moments of wavering willpower. You may need an encouraging SMS or a telephone call before you exercise. Work out how your friend can support you with your triggers to avoid, and set in motion a plan that includes their help. You can reassure them you'll just need their help for the first few weeks or in moments of wavering willpower – so, for a maximum of nine months and a minimum of just eighteen days, the time it takes for a behaviour to become a habit. Most people find that they need their friend's support to get started over the first few weeks and only occasionally afterwards.

Sign up on the website beextraordinarybook.com, and we will send you encouraging reminders to keep you going.

Does it come easier for some people?

Resisting the impulse to give in and delay your gratification, such as deciding to watch TV after you've been to the gym rather than before, does come easier for some people.

You may be familiar with the marshmallow experiment scientists carried out with children in the early 1970s at Stanford University. Children aged three to five were led to a room where a treat of their choice, such as a cookie, marshmallow or pretzel was waiting. Children were told they could eat the marshmallow now, or if they waited for fifteen minutes, they would be rewarded with a second marshmallow. Follow-up studies found that children who were able to wait performed better on scholastic aptitude tests and coped better with stress and frustration in later life.

But the little nugget that is not often mentioned about these findings is that a child's home environment is an important factor in determining whether or not they are able to delay eating their marshmallow. When this experiment was repeated with over 900 children from different backgrounds, the main finding that emerged was that children from deprived backgrounds had a tougher time delaying gratification. This finding is logical. If food is scarce at home, there's no benefit to delaying gratification. Eat when you can because it might not be there later on. A young child has not yet developed the sophisticated reasoning skills of an adult, and is unable to tell themselves that the research environment is different to their home environment. They can't reason with themselves that it's safe to wait fifteen minutes before scoffing marshmallows, that there really will be more in fifteen minutes.

Whilst a four-year-old may lack the capacity to reason with themselves and struggle to delay gratification, the good news is that your cognitive abilities are fully developed and you can remind yourself of the benefits of delaying a reward.

You may find it reassuring that many three-year-old children can delay their deepest desire to eat a yummy marshmallow in order to eat more marshmallows in fifteen minutes and so you too can delay watching TV, drinking hot chocolate or some other reward until after you've carried out the behaviour you're struggling to start.

Common obstacles

The couch

Doing nothing but falling into the comfort of your couch may be enjoyable in the short term, but in the long term it will keep feelings of guilt, disappointment and self-criticism going, which will only serve to make you feel badly about yourself and stop you from being your best.

Of course, we all love to lounge in front of the TV and of course, extraordinary people do this from time to time. But what helps them to emerge from inertia is not thoughts of how they will feel in the short term if they watch another box set, but how they will feel in the long term if they don't try their new behaviour, if they don't take a step towards the goal they're most passionate about today. It comes back to *future-feeling thinking*. Whether you are three or seventy-three being able to make decisions based on how you want to feel rather than on how you are feeling is the key to success when you are trying to help a healthy habit to stick.

How did Caroline cross the start line?

There is no substance more addictive than heroin. Some experts say that it hooks users from the first try.

Caroline first made a decision to get clean. This led to a cycle of stopping and starting, which lasted about a year. She was terrified to check into a methadone clinic because she believed she would lose custody of her daughter. She had been working as a prostitute to pay for her habit and had become close to a gay man, Eric, whom she respected very much. Sadly, he contracted HIV and AIDS. Caroline looked after him while he was dying. He had great belief in her strength as a compassionate, knowledgeable individual and he encouraged her to give up drugs and to study nursing. After several unsuccessful attempts to quit heroin for good, Caroline decided she had to *remove herself from her triggers*. She had been living in a heroin den with dealers, guns and friends who were using heavily. The temptation to start again was strong. So, she moved away. She cut all contact with her former friends.

In periods of intense craving, she reminded herself *why it was important* to stay off heroin, that she had a little girl who adored her every move and whom she loved deeply. She had a dear friend whose life had been cut tragically short, who wanted so much more for her, and who believed that she deserved much more than what lay ahead if she stuck with heroin.

She *recalled* Eric's desire for her to live a better life and his belief that she could do it. She brought to mind an *image* of Eric encouraging her, reassuring her she could do it and this strengthened her own belief that perhaps she could. With a clear mind, she gained insight into why she had been using. She had always thought her heroin use was a behaviour that said 'piss off to the world' but she realised in using she had been saying 'piss off' *to herself* and the opportunity to live an enriching life. She chose new behaviours to support living life without heroin; one of them was a *behaviour buddy* in the form of Narcotics Anonymous.

Caroline learned to spot the external and internal triggers that drove her to want to escape through heroin. She had successfully removed herself from the external triggers. The internal triggers, she realised, were linked to feeling angry and unworthy. When she felt angry, she learned to take extra-special care of herself rather than treating herself and others more harshly. She used her anger as a cue to be gentle with herself and to do more, rather than fewer, energy-enriching behaviours, such as eating well and sleeping early. She would call her sponsor or go to a meeting. She said that over time she discovered that difficult feelings pass. Caroline says, 'Even some days now, I can feel angry or quite down, and I say to myself that this is today, and tomorrow will be different.' When Caroline felt unworthy and wished to withdraw from the world, she used this feeling of wanting to escape as a sign to reach out to other people rather than withdraw, to go out of her way to connect rather than to avoid.

The 'I'm busy' obstacle

Manage your energy

To deal with daily commitments, consider energy management rather than time management. Prioritise tasks and your passions that require your focus when you have the most energy and your mundane tasks, such as paying bills or cleaning the dishes, during periods of low energy. During these times, practise *future-feeling thinking*, motivating yourself with the reward of feeling a sense of achievement, happiness, satisfaction and boosts in energy afterwards.

Boosts in energy can also help you start a mundane task. We achieve much more when we are feeling happy and positive, so consider fuelling your emotional energy to get you started.

A sure-fire way to help you feel instantly more positive and energised is to tell someone what you appreciate about them. This helps to transform your thinking. When we are focused on what we appreciate about someone else, even if we do not tell them, we begin to think with fewer negative words, which is linked to improvements in mood. Another proven method is to write down three good things, however small, that happened during the day. These could range from 'the post arrived on time' to 'the sun came out after lunch' or 'I made it to the gym'. For each of the three things that you noticed, answer the question, 'Why did the good thing happen?' Research shows that this writing exercise helps to lift mood and is linked to less depression up to three months later.

Most importantly, give the task your full attention. The more you can focus on what you are actually doing, the faster you'll complete the task and the happier you'll feel while doing it.

3. Avoidance Triggers

Before you can kick avoidance for good, you need to discover your avoidance triggers. Your triggers may be a mixture of thoughts, feelings, behaviours, people or your surroundings.

Thoughts

Two types of thoughts are likely to lead you to avoid the task you're meant to start: 'should' and 'temptation' thoughts. We've covered 'should' thoughts earlier in this chapter. Any thought with the word 'should' is going to trigger a desire to avoid. But 'temptation' thoughts are just as compelling. These are the kinds of thoughts that addicts face when they crave a substance. These thoughts tempt you away from the task you had planned. Thoughts such as 'I deserve . . .', 'It won't make a difference if . . .', 'One more won't hurt', 'I can always start again tomorrow', and so on.

The best way to spot your trigger thoughts is to think of the last time you planned an activity that you then avoided. Perhaps it was to join an exercise class at the gym or meet a friend for coffee. But on the day, you changed your mind. In the lead-up to deciding not to go, what went through your mind?

Below are examples of Caroline's thoughts when her mind suggested that she skip a meeting:

- 'I'm doing really well. I don't need to go.'

- 'I feel tired. I deserve to relax rather than go out into the cold and listen to two hours of the same old stuff.'

- 'I can't be bothered. I can always go tomorrow.'

- 'I should spend time with my daughter.'

What types of thoughts are likely to cause you to avoid? Make a note in your notebook or online journal.

Feelings

Thinking about the last time you avoided an activity you had planned, what were you feeling in the run-up to deciding not to go? Perhaps you were feeling flat, unmotivated or down. Perhaps your body felt tired.

Here are the feelings Caroline spotted when she felt like avoiding a meeting:

- 'I feel annoyed that I have to do this.'

- 'I feel tired.'

- 'I feel no motivation whatsoever.'

- 'I feel guilty I'm not spending more time with my daughter.'

- 'I feel down, unworthy. I'll go when I feel better.'

List the feelings you've spotted linked to your example of avoidance.

Behaviours

What were you doing in the run-up to making the decision to avoid the activity you had planned? Perhaps you were enjoying watching TV at home or perhaps you had just left work and were walking to your car.

Here is what Caroline spotted as trigger behaviours linked to the desire to avoid a meeting:

- 'Walking home from work, thinking about the patients who were sick and not going to get better.'

- 'Travelling to work, thinking about how I don't fit in at work.'

- 'Snuggling on the couch with my daughter not wanting the moment to end.'

You may notice that Caroline's trigger behaviours came into play close to home or close to work. They also involved the behaviour of thinking. What behaviours are holding you back? Are some of your behaviours linked to thinking?

People

Are there any people who may trigger your avoidance? It could be a friend you like to hang out with or your partner who offers a comforting cuddle and laughs. When you last skipped something you had planned to do were you tempted by the company of someone else?

There is one person who triggered Caroline's avoidance:

- 'My good friend, Hannah, who is still using.'

Surroundings

Thinking about the last time you avoided an activity you had planned, where were you? What were your surroundings?

The surrounding most likely to trigger Caroline's avoidance was the comfort of her own home. What are the surroundings most likely to tempt you away from an activity you had planned?

4. Overcoming Your Avoidance Triggers

It is your own self-talk that will ultimately help or hinder you. Therefore, the first step to overcoming your triggers is to respond to your thoughts. Let's look at how Caroline did this. She had a lot of 'temptation' thoughts: 'I'm doing really well. I don't need to go', 'I can't be bothered. I can always go tomorrow', 'I deserve to relax', and so on. She also had 'should' thoughts, which sparked an immediate desire to avoid. Caroline's should thoughts – 'I should spend more time with my daughter' – were more troublesome than her 'temptation' thoughts because they made her feel guilty. Guilt is a tricky emotion because it makes us feel badly about ourselves. When we feel badly about ourselves, we are more at risk of engaging in self-destructive behaviours, such as avoidance.

To overcome the pull to avoid, Caroline had to answer her trigger thoughts and remind herself of the bigger picture, why she was giving up heroin: to give her daughter a better life and a healthier, more present mother, and to be respectful to her deceased friend's image of her best future.

How Caroline answered her trigger thoughts

'I'm doing really well. I don't need to go.' I am doing well and going to a meeting will make me even stronger. The early days of abstinence are the hardest. What I risk by avoiding my meeting is slipping into a pattern where I give in. Giving in to these thoughts could mean giving in to heroin at some point in the future. I don't want this for me or for my daughter.

'I feel tired. I deserve to relax rather than get out into the cold and listen to two hours of the same old stuff.' Feeling tired is a sign that I need to take care of myself. The best way to take care of myself is to go to a meeting. I always feel more awake and happier after a meeting. Focusing on how I *will* feel rather than on how I *am* feeling will make it easier to get to the meeting.

'I can't be bothered. I can always go tomorrow.' It will be harder to go tomorrow if I avoid going today. I do care about my health, my daughter and being a sign of strength for her. Avoiding the meeting would be a step on the slippery slope back to using heroin. I don't want to let myself or my daughter down.

'I should spend time with my daughter.' I need to be alive and free of heroin for my daughter. This is far more important than being unavailable for two hours. Although it may seem that skipping the meeting and spending time with Louise would be in her best interest tonight, the reality is that the choices I make today affect my daughter for the rest of her life. If I skip a meeting and slip into heroin use, I risk losing her, I risk being unable to show her how extraordinary I can be, and how extraordinary she can be.

Then Caroline made a flashcard to remind herself why she had chosen to give up heroin.

> *Why am I giving up heroin?*
>
> I have a beautiful little girl, Louise, whom I love with every fibre in my body. Louise is only 6, a little wisp of a girl who needs care and love. She adores my every move, she looks to me for guidance, advice and love. What role model will I be if I give in to heroin? What will my drug behaviour show her about the world, about me? Louise deserves an extraordinary mother, a mother who can guide her to lead her own extraordinary life, a life where she is free to make choices based on dreams rather than worries about her mum. And there is Eric, too. He believed I had the capacity

to learn nursing and help people with health problems. I gave up heroin so I could be a better mum and so I could create an opportunity to explore Eric's best vision for me. None of this will be possible if I keep using.

Caroline looked at her flashcard several times a day, particularly when the temptation to avoid meetings or to use was strong. She also looked at a photo of Eric and she would play with Louise if she was home or look at a photo of her if she was at work. These were all tangible reminders of why she had chosen to give up heroin and try new behaviours, such as going to meetings, instead of using.

All of our triggers to avoid, whether they are thoughts, behaviours, feelings, surroundings or people, are warning signs that we need to give ourselves more, rather than less, care. Triggers are a sign to take extra care of yourself because they make you more vulnerable rather than more wilful.

> **Triggers are a sign to take extra care of yourself because they increase your vulnerability rather than your willpower.**

How did Caroline do it?

Caroline had strategies in place to deal with the behaviours and people linked to avoidance: she cut off contact with anyone who was still using, and she called her behaviour buddy, her NA sponsor, who supported her to get to meetings. Walking home from work or walking to work, depending on which thoughts filled her mind, was a trigger for Caroline. She addressed her thinking during these times, reminding herself of the bigger picture, and she thought of Louise and Eric. Sometimes she would take a different route home, through the park rather than through the high street. Walking through the park, she would focus on what she could hear and see, on the first spring flowers, the sound of chirping birds and on the dandelion buttoning the lawn. She would imagine her friend, Eric, and the walks he had taken in the very same park, the path his feet had walked along, the trees he had seen, the grass he had lain on, the birdsong he had enjoyed and the air he had breathed in and out, in the same park where she was breathing now. When Caroline focused on sharing the same air, on touching the same path and seeing the same trees, she felt closer to him and the future he had held for her and this strengthened her determination to stay clean. Shifting her attention away from her thinking to what she was seeing and hearing helped Caroline to overcome the pull of 'should' and 'temptation' thoughts.

Ironically, Caroline's most vulnerable surrounding was being at home. Although her home with her daughter, Louise, was very different to the drug den she had been living in, the surroundings triggered 'should' and 'temptation' thoughts after a day of work when she felt tired. Recognising that her home was likely to trigger wavering willpower, Caroline took steps to create an environment that would support her goal: staying clean. She put up lots of photos of Louise and her doing activities they had been able to start once she was clean, like swimming together, a visit to the zoo and a shot inside a science museum. She also put out photos of places she wanted to visit with Louise that she would only be able to do if she was clean, such as Paris, and three local craft fair leaflets which offered art classes for kids in the summer. Caroline also got good at challenging her 'should' and 'temptation' thoughts when she was at home.

Finally, Caroline addressed the feelings linked to avoiding. When she was feeling tired, angry or unworthy, unmotivated or guilty, she showed herself compassion, reminded herself of how far she had come, and again, why she was choosing new behaviours. She used her feeling, her deep desire to escape as a sign to reach out to her behaviour buddy or her NA sponsor rather than withdraw. She made plans to socialise, to connect with other people, or go to a meeting rather than avoid.

With these steps, Caroline overcame addiction to heroin. She overcame the temptation to give in. She overcame the desire to sink into the couch and her past. Caroline took care of herself, which created opportunity for her to begin to follow her dreams, her vision of working in health care, drawing on the strength she had gained from overcoming the world's most addictive substance by herself.

Triggers are a sign to take care of yourself, an opportunity to spot and respond to thoughts, behaviours, feelings, people, and surroundings that may be keeping avoidance in place. Like Caroline, you can talk back to thoughts that will tempt you to stay stuck in a rut. You can practise *future-feeling thinking*, making decisions that will support a new behaviour based on how you will feel afterwards rather than on how you are feeling beforehand. You can remind yourself why your new behaviour is important to you and you can imagine the times you have tried it to encourage you to keep going. Like Caroline, you'll need to remove yourself from people who may draw you to avoid and like Caroline, you may need to pay extra special attention to your surroundings. If the comfort of your couch makes it more likely that you'll stay put, then don't sit down. Or, put your gym gear on the couch (if it's exercise you're keen to start) or even a photo of you achieving the new behaviour.

Transforming avoidance into action is a great way to take care of yourself and put you on the path to extraordinary.

How else can you take care of yourself? Four behaviours support extraordinary health, which in turn will strengthen your resolve to kick avoidance for good.

5. Taking Care of Yourself

Get sweaty

The first is exercise. Get sweaty. Exercise detoxes the body of depressive chemicals and reduces insulin resistance and inflammation, both of which are linked to memory problems in later life. Exercise stimulates the growth of new blood cells and the release of chemicals that keep brain cells healthy. In short, exercise boosts your mood and brain function so much that the UK National Institute for Health and Care Excellence recommends exercise as a treatment for mild to moderate depression. The latest studies now know exactly how exercise works to keep us happy.

When we exercise, a protein that controls the genes linked to energy metabolism increases in skeletal muscles. The protein, called PGC-1alpha1, produces an enzyme that turns harmful kynurenine, a by-product of tryptophan metabolism, into kynurenic acid, which the body can easily pass.

We saw in Chapter IV that tryptophan is an amino acid, found in protein like turkey, which gets converted to serotonin in the brain. Serotonin is a feel-good chemical, mostly found in our digestive tracts but also in our blood and central nervous system.

Exercise seems to help our muscles clear out harmful depressive chemicals, which may increase the bioavailability of serotonin, boosting our feel-good feelings.

Cardiovascular exercise, like running or cycling, and endurance training are the types of exercise most likely to be helpful. This kind of exercise increases enzymes in muscles necessary to convert harmful kynurenine to kynurenic acid, which cannot pass the blood brain barrier, a cellular border that protects the brain from pathogens circulating in the blood. Reducing kynurenine in the blood protects the brain from stress-induced changes linked to depression.

Get savvy about sleep

The second behaviour to support extraordinary health is sleep. A good night's sleep is linked to better mood, memory and immunity. Scientists have discovered that during sleep the space between cells increases, which may help the brain to flush out toxins. It may help to explain why we feel physically and emotionally drained after a few days of little sleep.

Sleep activates a plumbing system called the glymphatic system that helps fluid to move rapidly through the brain. When scientists injected mice with beta-amyloid, a protein that builds up in the brains of people affected by Alzheimer's disease, the brains of sleeping mice cleared it much faster than those who were awake, leading experts to conclude that sleep helps to clear toxic molecules from the brain.

Over time, poor sleep creates a chronic sleep debt that has harmful effects on carbohydrate metabolism and hormone health, similar to those seen in age-related disorders. Poor sleep also makes it tougher to change thoughts linked to negative feelings, which means the amygdala, our fear centre, stays active for longer.

The take-home message from the accumulating research on the harmful effects of sleep debt underscores the importance of getting your sleep in order. Try to get to bed before midnight and up before 8 a.m. Sleep in a dark room. Avoid caffeine in the evening and limit your alcohol and chocolate after dinner. Invest in a comfortable mattress and be kind to yourself. Accept that as you age, your sleep quantity will shorten, and you'll sleep less deeply. Adjust your expectations of sleep quality. Avoid worrying about how much sleep you achieve and instead focus on how to manage your energy during the day, knowing that if you've skimped on sleep one night, you'll likely sleep more deeply the next night, something to look forward to after a poor night's sleep.

Plan ahead

The third gem for supporting extraordinary health is planning ahead, a simple tool that takes ten minutes a day. Several studies show that making a plan in the evening for the next day and including one enjoyable activity in your plan dramatically improves mood and well-being. We asked student paramedics to create a plan in the evening for the next day. They had to link a task or activity to a time during the day, such as 'at 5 a.m., I'll shower then eat breakfast, 6 a.m. start shift, 1 p.m. finish shift, have protein snack, 2 p.m. hit the gym, 3 p.m. steam room and shower, 4 p.m. food shopping, 5 p.m. make dinner, eat and tidy up, 7 p.m. watch Netflix, 9 p.m. bed.' Another group of paramedics were asked to read about mental health rather than plan their next day and a third group of paramedics didn't have to do anything. The paramedics who planned ahead had dramatically better well-being at the end of the study. They also reported much less psychological distress. We've repeated this study a few times with different groups of people and have consistently replicated the results.

We think planning ahead works because it reduces opportunity to worry, which means it may improve sleep. Also, including a fun activity in your plan makes it more likely that you'll do something fun, which, of course, is going to increase feelings of well-being. Having a detailed plan of what you'll do the next day may also make you more productive, meaning you'll be more likely to reach your goals.

Be kind to your mind

The fourth behaviour that will guide you to transition from ordinary to extraordinary health is compassionate thinking and speaking. Speaking to yourself with kindness rather than criticism lowers stress hormones and promotes optimism. Whilst it may feel unnatural to speak to yourself with kindness, it probably doesn't feel unnatural when you're speaking to a friend. So, the next time your mind fills with self-critical self-talk, spot the opportunity to extend the same kindness you offer others to yourself. Instead of chastising yourself for missing the gym, imagine what you would say to a friend, especially now that you're equipped with the knowledge of how to transform avoidance and kick-start a new habit. Instead of saying to yourself: 'I'm such a useless, lazy idiot for not getting to the gym' you could try, 'I now know that feeling tired is one of my triggers for avoidance and I have to take more rather than less care of myself around my triggers. I'm likely to feel tired after work again tomorrow so I'll ask Lindsay to call me then to give me a bit of encouragement. I'll also take a moment to connect with how I will feel after I've been to the gym as motivation to get myself there. And, of course, I'll remind myself of why it's important to me to go to the gym. I want to be fit enough to go on that sailing trip with my husband.'

Self-critical talk zaps motivation whereas kind and compassionate self-talk encourages problem-solving and more action. If you're struggling to speak to yourself with kindness, you could first try to think kind thoughts or carry out kind gestures for other people. The act of being kind will boost your mood and put you in a frame of mind where it's easier for you to be kind to yourself.

How Can You Take This Forward?

Avoidance is the number-one unhelpful behaviour that will keep you stuck in a rut. In this chapter, we looked at how to kick avoidance. We learned from Caroline, a young woman who overcame addiction to heroin, the world's most addictive drug, by herself. We discovered how 'should' and 'temptation' thoughts drive avoidance, and we covered how to spot triggers linked to avoidance. These include a mixture of thoughts, feelings, behaviours, surroundings and people. We discovered how Caroline responded to her triggers to use heroin and how to apply this learning to our own lives. We also learned about four key behaviours that support extraordinary health and have the potential to strengthen our resolve to kick avoidance. Which new behaviours are you keen to start? What are your triggers to avoid? Use the techniques described in this chapter to banish avoidance and kick-start new behaviours to zoom you forward on your path to extraordinary.

In a Nutshell

Avoidance is the number-one unhelpful behaviour that will keep you stuck in a rut.

Two types of thoughts increase the likelihood that you'll avoid: 'should' and 'temptation' thoughts.

'Should' thoughts kick-start a desire to avoid. 'I should go to the gym' is an example of a 'should' thought.

'Temptation' thoughts are excuses to give in. 'I'm doing really well. I don't need to go to the gym' is an example of a temptation thought.

When you notice a 'should' or 'temptation' thought come to mind, replace it with a question: how will I feel after I've tried my new behaviour?

Be guided by how you want to feel rather than by how you are feeling. This is *future-feeling thinking*, making decisions to act based on how you want to feel in the future rather than on how you are feeling now.

You need to try your new behaviour just once to kick-start a new habit and anywhere from 18 to 264 days to make it automatic.

Nine tips will help you start a new behaviour
- The three-minute carrot gives you permission to quit or keep going after trying something for three minutes
- Allow yourself to do an average rather than a perfect job
- Schedule the new behaviour with a friend
- Schedule a reward for once you've achieved your new behaviour

- List the reasons why the new behaviour is important to you
- Picture success: imagine having achieved your new behaviour
- Take a selfie once you've tried the new behaviour. Seeing you achieving it is great motivation to try it again
- Enlist the help of a behaviour buddy
- Manage your energy. Schedule your new behaviour when you have energy. Do your mundane stuff when you have dips in energy

Spot and respond to your triggers to avoid. These include a mixture of thoughts, feelings, behaviours, people and surroundings.

Take care of yourself
- Get sweaty with cardiovascular exercise like running or cycling or endurance training
- Get savvy about sleep
- Plan ahead. Make a plan in the evening for the next day. Include one enjoyable activity in your plan
- Be kind to your mind. Extend the same kindness you offer others to yourself

VI.

Determination

When we think of extraordinary people, we think of their incredible accomplishments, their vision and their determination. We know that many of the most extraordinary and successful people in the world faced challenges. Nelson Mandela was imprisoned; Steve Jobs was put up for adoption as a baby and was a college dropout.

But we rarely think about how these people endured and overcame such challenges. How did they maintain determination in the face of persistent obstacles? How did they keep a positive attitude in the face of injustice or rejection?

It can be easy to assume that these famous people had some innate superpower that simply enabled them to endure harsh circumstances. But ordinary people who transition to extraordinary use determination on a daily basis too to overcome negative circumstances and build a better life. Take Charlotte, for example.

Charlotte suffered early separation from her family, life-threatening illness, bereavement, job loss, then career loss, and two long drawn-out divorces. She emerged with her resolve intact, returned to university in her forties, and within months of graduating had started a thriving world-class bioscience company.

In this chapter, we'll look at how to maintain your momentum on your path to success. Here we'll learn the difference between determination and motivation. We'll discover how to pick up momentum and run with your big vision, even in the face of defeat. People who transition from ordinary to extraordinary with trauma as their catalyst redefine responses to rejection. They're motivated to start and determined to keep going. They learn from challenges and they push through unbelievable setbacks to create success.

1. What is Determination?

Determination is the inner grit that keeps you in for the long haul, that connects you to your bigger vision and weaves your capacity to problem-solve into your track for success.

Do you need motivation to transition from ordinary to extraordinary? Absolutely. Motivation is the key to taking your first step. But it is determination that will keep you going.

It is a lot like running a marathon

Your bigger vision is a lot like running a marathon. It requires planning, it may require training, a course here or there. It will require a sizeable amount of your time. It certainly requires the motivation to start and most definitely the determination to keep going – even when you feel unmotivated, tired, sore and fed up.

2. How do I strengthen the motivation to start?

Motivation relies on reward-based learning, which is heavily linked to your brain's capacity to synthesise dopamine. When you start and finish a task on your to-do list, your brain releases a burst of dopamine, which rewards you. It's a chemical pat on the back and makes you feel good. Your brain associates completing tasks with feeling good, which entices you to finish them. The fact that you achieve more by doing more is a side effect of reward-based learning. Completion of the first step is what gets and keeps you going because of the link between finishing a task and feeling good.

We can learn a lot about motivation from things that kill motivation. Picture a troubled teenager, intent on shutting himself from the world, lounging in his bedroom, clouds of smoke wafting through the air as he puffs a joint, drifting to a far-off place. Whilst he may think he's chilling in the cool zone, feeling the music he's listening to or rewarding his developing brain, what he's really doing is killing his motivation. And if he does this for long enough, he'll kill his motivation for good, making it hard to get going. There's a clear link between cannabis use and what's called amotivational syndrome or lack of motivation, which tells us an awful lot about how motivation works.

> Taking the first step unlocks the likelihood that you'll keep going.

The specific mechanism through which motivation dissipates with heavy cannabis use is precisely what tells us how to kick-start motivation. Chronic, heavy cannabis use impairs dopamine synthesis, which means it disrupts reward-based learning.

In a ground-breaking study looking at the link between cannabis use and motivation, over 500 college students filled in questionnaires about substance use, personality and self-efficacy (the capacity to tap initiative and reach goals) at two time points separated by a month. Using sophisticated statistics, the researchers were able to determine that heavy cannabis use reduces levels of self-efficacy and that the opposite was not true, that low levels of self-efficacy do not necessarily lead to heavy cannabis use. So, it's not feeling a lack of confidence in one's ability to reach goals that leads to cannabis use, but rather heavy cannabis use that blocks the capacity to tap initiative and get going. What this means is that motivation has to do with your capacity to start a task. If you can take the first step, you'll likely keep going. The key is to take that first step.

The first step

The last chapter gave a lot of tools to help you cross the start line without pressuring you to reach the finish line. The one that works best for my clients is the three-minute carrot – it's easy to start something for three minutes and then give yourself permission to stop or to keep going. Most people decide after three minutes to keep going because they discover, once they've started, that it doesn't feel as tough as they thought it would.

If you need to break your first step into tiny tasks to get started, do it. It's manageable to complete a small step like 'write an outline for my business plan' before the bigger step 'write the background section'. Completing the small step gives a sense of achievement, motivating next steps.

We saw in Chapter V that striving for perfection can stop you from starting – and that giving yourself permission to do an okay job or even a bad job makes it easier to start because everyone can do something badly. You may remember the client from the last chapter who wanted to make flossing a regular habit? To start, she gave herself permission to miss teeth, to do a bad job, but to bring flossing into her daily routine. She flossed every day for three weeks, missing teeth and generally doing a poor job. After three weeks, she upped her target to 'floss every tooth'. Since she already had twenty-one days of flossing under her belt, the shift from poor flossing to proper flossing was seamless. The real challenge had been to make it a part of her routine. Once it was a daily habit, it was fairly straightforward to floss well. She discovered that flossing correctly took no more time than flossing poorly.

Pursue your passion

It goes without saying that the more passionate you are about your bigger vision, the more motivated you'll be to take your first steps and the more committed to pursuing them. Creating your bigger vision with the questions in Chapter 1 first guided you to spot moments that had really knocked your socks off and to look at what leading an extraordinary life would mean to you – what could be extraordinary for you? This was for the purpose of creating a long-term vision that encapsulated excitement, energy and your own meaning of extraordinary. You'll be keener to work towards your bigger vision when it combines passion and depth – the meaning of extraordinary for you, which will naturally be exciting to you.

Charlotte's Story

Charlotte is an American woman born into upper-middle-class wealth. She enjoyed an idyllic childhood with her grandparents on a West Country farm in England while her parents built their business in the US. When she was four years old, the family business was thriving and her grandparents sent her back to live with them. By the time she was a teenager, the family had lost their fortune through a bitter divorce, and Charlotte had developed glandular fever followed by encephalitis, almost dying. Charlotte recovered yet was left with chronic migraines. She took up work selling ice creams to help make ends meet whilst she finished high school. She could not cope with the ongoing health issues, working part time and her full-time studies so when she was just nineteen years old she started then dropped out of university and moved to the East coast for a better life. She married, only to discover that her husband was an alcoholic. After four years, Charlotte mustered her strength, applied for a scholarship to an Ivy League university and left her husband to pursue a degree in Russian Language and Literature.

When Charlotte graduated, she translated documents from Russian to English for a small legal firm that soon went bust. Suddenly jobless, Charlotte moved to the UK to pursue more promising opportunities in translating only to discover upon arriving that her grandfather was dying. She gave up her early career to care for him. She met a TV film and set designer and married again. Charlotte began writing and selling film scripts. She directed one of her scripts, which won the Independent Film Awards' Best Short Film. Thrilled, Charlotte wrote a romantic comedy feature film, which attracted tremendous interest. But no funding. She divorced whilst continuing to write and sell scripts. After ten years of unsuccessful attempts to secure funding for her romantic comedy, Charlotte left the film industry. She returned to university to start again in another direction. Pursuing her passion for science, Charlotte applied to the University of Oxford's MSc programme in Clinical Pharmacology. She was short-listed for interview but told a place on the programme was unlikely because she did not hold a formal science background.

Determined, Charlotte met with the head of department and members of the admissions committee for interview. She blew them away with her science knowledge, immediately securing a place on the programme. Charlotte graduated with distinction and started a thriving bioscience company whose profit is now funding the romantic comedy she had dreamed of directing and producing.

3. How Do I Build My Determination Muscle?

After the first step

You've taken your first step and unlocked the likelihood that you'll keep going. Now what?

What else can help? Are there certain kinds of steps that are better than others?

In a nutshell, yes. Steps that lead to results keep you going. For example, one of your steps may be to search online for courses on starting a business. You have control over this and reaching the outcome is within your control, which gives satisfaction on achieving it and readies you for the next step.

But if one of your steps is booking a meeting with an expert in the field, to some degree this is out of your control. You can fire off the email to make contact (well done), but you rely on someone else to complete this step, someone else's response to your email. If you don't hear from the other person, you can't complete the step, which can dampen motivation. So, it's important when you schedule your bullet points of tasks and steps for your bigger vision that you also include tasks that are completely within your control. Achieving these tasks keeps you going and gives you the will to problem-solve the tasks that are out of your control.

The 'just-right' challenge

You may remember in Chapter III, Focus, hearing about a researcher with a long name – Mihaly Csikszentmihalyi. He's most cited for the counter-intuitive finding that what makes people happiest is to be absorbed in something challenging enough to be stimulating, but not so challenging that it's frustrating. What this means is . . . break tasks into stimulating steps where possible. Instead of scheduling some-thing rather overwhelming, like 'write business plan for a children's thrive-with-reading programme', break this into smaller steps that include interesting ones – like, 'read Winowa's business plan for her children's poetry company', 'watch a Ted talk on changing education programmes', 'write the outline for my business plan and schedule when to write the content for the Background', and other headings.

Dealing with decisions

Making a lot of decisions zaps the power to focus. We saw in Chapter III that people did better on an attention and memory task when they had walked in a park first rather than navigating the streets of downtown Michigan. Why? Navigating the streets required them to make a lot of decisions: how to cross the road without getting hit by traffic or tourists, which street to take to reach their final destination, how to avoid bumping pedestrians, and so on. People performed poorly after downtown walking because they had zapped their attention with multiple mundane decisions, making it tough to focus when they needed to.

The meaning of this finding – save your brain power for tough daytime decisions. Remove the mundane decisions to the night before. As I teach on my resilience courses, the night before is the best time to plan the next day – decide how you'll allocate your time, to which tasks, when you'll take a break and what you'll do for your break. You can also store up mental energy for harder tasks by deciding the night before: what you'll wear the next day, what you'll eat and how you'll travel to wherever you need to go.

Dealing with opportunities

As you progress in your career, lots of opportunities will come your way. It is tempting to say 'yes' to that extra speaking engagement, the short-notice workshop, the request to synthesise the results of the latest research in your field of expertise. Pretty soon, you'll be running ragged with your attention spread thin, finding no time to step towards your long-term goals. It's natural as you progress towards success that you receive more requests for work. And it is easy to get side-lined and off track with interesting but less relevant projects. Remember, people who transition from ordinary to extraordinary with trauma as their catalyst have learned the value of time. Our todays may not be our tomorrows. So, when opportunities come your way that may take time from your bigger vision, ask yourself: Will this opportunity benefit me in some way? Will it take me closer or further away from my big vision? The answer to this question will help you to decide whether or not to push towards completing an extra piece of work which may have no benefit (other than extra cash) to you or your long-term goals.

Dealing with obstacles

It's inevitable as you make progress with your bigger vision that you'll hear the word 'no'. 'No', the investors are not investing in your start-up. 'No', your application for funding was not accepted. 'No', the editor of your favourite magazine is not publishing your piece. 'No', your perfect potential business partner doesn't want to start a business with you. What then?

People who transition from ordinary to extraordinary with or without trauma as their catalyst redefine responses to 'no'. 'No' does not mean stopping in your tracks and kissing your dreams goodbye. 'No' means 'try another avenue', 'problem-solve', 'readjust your plan' or 'ask for help'.

After ten years of slogging it out in the film industry, receiving promises for funding but no solid backing, Charlotte decided to take another route to producing her romantic comedy. She completely restarted with a new career, returning to university to gain the necessary qualification to back her bioscience company. With the profit her company earns, she is now producing her romantic comedy. She had her big vision, it was unchanging; what did change was her route to get there.

Kenny, whom you read about in Chapter I, Vision, dreamed of being a personal trainer. But he was almost blind after his trauma. When he applied for his sports science qualification he was told that it would be too dangerous for him to work with weights, especially with other people. He set out to prove how safe he was. And he did. He achieved his qualification and kept going, working so well that his business helping injured people to achieve their fitness goals expanded to include people of all abilities.

Afet, whom you'll read about in the next chapter, lost her legs as a result of a severe infection she picked up in hospital. Afet told herself that she walked into hospital and there was no way on Earth she wouldn't be walking out of hospital. After four surgeries and six months of rehab, Afet indeed walked out of hospital on two prosthetic legs.

'No' does not mean it's impossible. It means try another route.

Putting your head together with people who matter

When you hear of the achievements of Steve Jobs, Nelson Mandela or other famous extraordinary people, you likely recognise that their milestones were achieved with the help of teams of people putting their heads together to solve problems that arose on the path to extraordinary success. You too will benefit from putting your head together with like-minded people, who may have already achieved quite a bit in your field or who hold expertise you can call on or who are already working towards their greater vision. You may like to join the Be Extraordinary community on www.beex traordinarybook.com where you can buddy up with other project leaders, learn a few tips in your trade and receive encouragement in the moments that matter.

Charlotte needed a qualification in clinical pharmacology to set up and run her bioscience company. When she met the admissions committee for her interview at Oxford University, what she was doing, to some degree, was putting her head together with people who matter to problem-solve the issue of not having a medical degree whilst still demonstrating the knowledge requirements for admission. She impressed with her knowledge in that meeting and they clearly problem-solved the issue that had arisen with her application.

Know what you need and ask for it

One of the benefits of linking your big vision to a clear plan is that you give yourself the opportunity to spot the steps and resources you'll need for your success. You have the opportunity to think through what courses might make your journey easier; who might make an inspiring, proactive mentor; how to structure your work day to give you an hour or so to work on your bigger vision, and so on. When you look at your week or month and schedule the tasks you need to achieve to move closer to your big vision, ask yourself what will increase the likelihood of achieving this step. Think in specifics. What do you need from your kids? A quiet hour a week? What do you need to hear from your partner? Some words of encouragement or something practical, like cooking a meal or two? What about your friends? What you do need from them? Is there any support your current employer could give you – such as working flexitime so you can reduce commuting time and devote the saved minutes to completing a task for your big vision?

Get clear on what you need and ask for it. This is far more helpful than complaining about not having enough time. Think through how much time you really need per week to devote to your big vision and work out how you can reliably carve out this time. If you need one hour a week, then perhaps your partner cooking three meals or you working flexitime to avoid commuting time may free up the hour you need. Use it wisely. Hire a coach in the short term if you need to. You can put your head together with a coach to work out what is feasible to achieve in your week.

Collaboration

In the compelling book *Sapiens: A Brief History of Humankind*, Yuval Noah Harari put forward a convincing case for how humans evolved, citing collaboration as one of the keys to our success as a species. Bottom line: collaborate. Reach out to people who have achieved something similar or experts in the area you're working in or people striving to achieve a meaningful big vision, read their blogs, make connections, immerse yourself in success. You'll be inspired to keep going with your own big vision. Collaborate on the parts of your projects that will benefit from two heads rather than one. Another like-minded person with a passion for your joint success can maintain the project's momentum and keep you thinking big.

Balance

It can be tough to take breaks when your time is spread thin and you're using all of it to work towards bringing your big vision to fruition. But you will need to balance work with breaks, or you risk burn-out, which is a precursor to depression. Burn-out will stop you in your tracks for months. Plan and take smart breaks: a walk in your garden or a park, prepping a healthy snack, watching an upbeat programme, a regular exercise class, enjoying an extra hour in bed, and so on. Look after yourself with the extraordinary behaviours we uncovered in Chapter V. The behaviours that support your physical health – scheduling exercise, healthy meals and good sleep – support you to make progress. Plan breaks in your day and days when you give yourself a break. Remember the 'just-right' challenge; make sure you're including many steps on your to-do list that are stimulating but not overwhelming.

Deadlines, the specifics and the science

Nothing focuses the mind like a deadline, a real one, one where you're accountable preferably to someone else like your kids, partner, mentor or coach. It's harder to let someone else down than ourselves. So set manageable deadlines and let a specific person know your plan.

Be specific in what you intend to achieve when you share your plans. Rather than saying, 'I intend to work regularly on my business plan', let your partner know that on Saturday afternoon at 2 p.m., you're writing the Background for your business plan. Why? The research shows that when we share our general (rather than specific) intentions and other people notice them, we work less hard.

Peter Gollwitzer and his team looked at the effect of sharing our intentions with others. They studied psychology and law students. If aspiring law students shared their intention 'I intend to make the best possible use of educational opportunities in law' and the experimenter noticed this on a questionnaire and they could see that the experimenter had spotted their intention, they spent less time working through criminal law cases in the study than if the experimenter had not noticed this intention. Equally, psychology students who expressed an intention to watch videotapes of therapy sessions to learn more about therapeutic techniques spent less time analysing the videos when the experimenter noticed rather than failed to notice their intention.

So, share specific intentions that you've linked to a deadline: 'I intend to take a break at 3 p.m. for a cup of tea and restart on the Budget section of my business plan at 3:30 p.m.' rather than general intentions like 'I intend to start a business plan.'

4. Dealing with Setbacks

Smart ways to deal with worry

When you face a setback, it's natural to worry about how to move forward. You may start to worry about whether or not you have what it takes to succeed. You may worry

> **Focus on facts not feelings to overcome worry.**

about the outcome of upcoming business meetings or networking events. You may worry about earning enough in the short term to support your bigger vision in the long term. You may worry about any number of possible problems. These could be legal, family, health or financial problems.

When worrying starts, it can spiral into full-blown self-doubt and despair. The best way out of this rut is to recognise what worry is: over-thinking and catastrophising. We covered these unhelpful thinking habits in Chapter IV, Get Out of Your Head. When people worry, they *over-think* what could happen, focusing on unanswerable 'what if' questions. 'What if the company turnover takes a nosedive?', 'What if the investors decide the idea is not up their alley?', 'What if the lottery funding doesn't come through?', 'What if it takes four years longer than we'd like?', and so on. Worrying, you will notice, leads to no plan or action. It is immensely unproductive and focuses your mind on the worst possible rather than likely outcomes. Worry, like dwelling, blocks the capacity to problem-solve. It's important to get on top of worrying before it gets on top of you.

Remember that *88 per cent of our worries never happen.* Keeping track of your worries will help you to collect your own evidence about how often your own worries fail to come true. This will guide you to rely on facts rather than feelings when you're thinking about future events.

I like the worry diary that leading worry experts Tom Borkovec and Colette Hirsch developed. It asks you to note your worry, the outcome and how well you coped. Here is an example of the diary that a client has completed. You can use it too to keep track of your main worries.

Situation	My worry	Actual outcome	Worry came true?	How well I coped? 0–10
Pitching business idea to Matt's boss, a potential investor.	*Last pitch did not go well. Blanked on the finance question. I'll forget the numbers when I need to remember them. The idea will be demolished with criticism.*	*The pitch went like I practised – I remembered everything, including the company's turnover in each of the last 3 years. Matt's boss decided not to invest although he liked the idea. He gave great feedback on the pitch and my company, and said he really liked the idea, it's just not his area of expertise.*	*No*	*9*

Attending charity fund-raiser event.	It's an opportunity to network, mention my business. People won't be interested and will cut conversations short.	Actually, this didn't happen. There were lots of like-minded people at the event. It was inspiring and people took a keen interest in my business. I managed to give out 17 business cards.	No	10
Meet with current boss to pitch flexitime.	My boss will be annoyed I'm not devoting all my free time to his project. He will likely grant flexitime but only begrudgingly.	My boss did grant flexitime. He wasn't keen, though. But he understood the logic of my request and we agreed if my productivity changes, we'll reassess flexitime.	Yes	9
Meet client over lunch on Tuesday.	Discuss initial findings of my review. She'll push for faster progress.	Had a nice lunch with Saskia. She was grateful for the initial findings and outlined how they'll help her make decisions with her team. She's looking forward to my final report. She wasn't pushy for more progress.	No	10

At the end of the week, you'll be able to calculate the percentage of your worries that did not come true. For example, if you note ten worries and nine never happened, then the percentage of your worries that never happened is 90 per cent. You'll also be able to gauge how well you coped with the worries that may have come true. We almost always cope better than we think we will.

Dealing with self-doubt

Realistic risk

When we doubt ourselves, we tend to remember the times we were less successful than we'd hoped. With memories where we failed to measure up filling our mind, we'll likely feel more rather than less doubtful of our capacity for success. The stronger our feelings of doubt, the more we'll lead ourselves to believe that failure is the only outcome. This is called *emotional reasoning*: using our feelings, rather than fact, to make predictions about what may happen.

> Using facts not feelings to make predictions about future events reduces anxiety and worry.

Believing that failure is the likely outcome will motivate more rather than fewer behaviours linked to failing: withdrawing, taking no action, letting things slide.

It is therefore important to focus on the actual likelihood of our doubts or worries coming true rather than on how much we feel like they're about to happen. We can do this with some number crunching.

For example, Charlotte worried that she'd stuff up, that she'd never reach her goal of producing her romantic comedy. She had written and directed a short black comedy, which had won the Best Short Film, but she had been unsuccessful in securing investment for the feature film she'd written. In moments of self-doubt, when she felt 100 per cent anxious and defeated, she believed with 100 per cent conviction that she'd never succeed with her romantic comedy or her bioscience company.

Emotional reasoning made Charlotte feel worse.

Realistic risk

To calculate the realistic risk of Charlotte failing, she first worked out how many goals she had set herself and how many goals she had failed.

Facts

Charlotte was 45 years old. She had set herself well over 200 goals in her life, starting at school, with goals to achieve As or Bs in each course she took in high school and university. This amounted to 64 goals. She had set herself personal goals as a teenager, such as winning horse-jumping events and progressing to black belt in Judo. As an adult, she had set herself personal goals of exercising thirty minutes three times a week, learning Russian, French and Spanish, and of learning to code. She had goals of rescuing injured animals, of writing and selling scripts, of directing a short film and, of course, of studying for a Master's in Clinical Pharmacology, of directing her rom com and of starting her bioscience company. Charlotte estimated that since the age of thirteen she had set herself about seven goals a year. She subtracted 13 from 45 (her current age) giving her 32 years of goal setting. She multiplied 32 by 7 yielding 224 goals. She worked out that so far there were 3 main goals she hadn't achieved: she had not achieved a black belt in Judo (she had progressed to brown belt), she exercised about once a week on average rather than three times a week and she had not secured funding for her romantic comedy.

The Stats

Number of goals Charlotte had not reached divided by
Number of goals Charlotte had set x 100%
= Charlotte's realistic risk of failing

$3/224 = 0.01 \times 100\% = 1\%$

The actual likelihood of Charlotte not reaching her goals, based on her own life experience, was 1 per cent. This is much lower than what her feelings had predicted, which had put her likelihood for failure at a whopping 100 per cent!

The likely outcome

The next step is to picture the likely outcome. Call to mind the winning image you worked on in Chapter I instead of what you fear will happen.

For instance, Charlotte had more examples of achieving rather than failing. You probably do, too. Whenever Charlotte had the thought that she wouldn't secure funding, she reminded herself of the likely outcome based on her own history of success and she called to mind her winning image, which was based on her photo of receiving the Independent Film Awards' Best Short Film. Then she refocused her attention on the task at hand to problem-solve the setback and move forward.

> **Using facts not feelings to make predictions about our capacity for success reduces self-doubt.**

Anything positive reduces worry

The latest science shows that thinking about anything positive reduces worry. Worry expert Colette Hirsch at King's College London ran a study where her team trained 102 volunteers with pathological levels of worry to replace their worries with images of positive outcomes or with verbal statements that captured the positive outcomes or to call to mind other positive images, such as a setting sun, that were unrelated to their worries. The researchers discovered that picturing or thinking something positive related or unrelated to volunteers' worries reduced their anxiety and helped them to disengage from worry during the study and in the longer term. The bottom line is that if you are worrying, call to mind a positive outcome that may or may not be related to your worry; it will help you to feel less anxious.

Extraordinary belief

When you face a setback like a rejected application for a needed qualification or an interview that flops, it's easy to doubt yourself. The problem with self-doubt is that it causes you to withdraw. When you withdraw, you become less active, making it more likely that you'll slip into a rut, and less likely you'll take a small step or any step towards your bigger vision, weakening rather than strengthening your resolve for success. The best way out of a setback is to call to mind your extraordinary belief, the one you worked on in Chapter I. Ask yourself: what would someone who is 100 per cent [insert your extraordinary belief] do in this situation? What would be their next step? For example, what would someone who is 100 per cent bright, organised, a problem-solver, a hard worker, and a kind person with grit do in this situation? What would [insert the people who most want you to succeed] suggest you do in this situation?

Extraordinary image

Hand in hand with your extraordinary belief comes your extraordinary image. Seeing the picture of you succeeding in your mind's eye, the image that encapsulates your extraordinary belief, will strengthen your confidence. Remember, picturing a positive image reduces worry and anxiety. The extraordinary image we worked on in Chapter I also includes the people who would most relish your success. These people know without a shadow of a doubt that you can do it. Picturing their kind faces strengthens your self-belief, and helps you to tap compassion, leading to more effective problem-solving. We saw in Chapter I that Sir Ranulph Fiennes, in moments of doubt and extreme danger, called to mind vivid images of his father and grandfather, two people he most aspired to make proud. These images kept him going in situations where most people would have quit.

Flexible and realistic expectations

Apply realistic expectations to scheduling tasks you'll take during the week towards your bigger vision. Expecting to work full time, raise your children and run a business in the evenings is . . . unrealistic. Of course, you can work full time, raise your children and start a business, but to do this without reaching burn-out requires realistic planning and setting flexible and realistic expectations for the moments you are free. You'll need to work out what resources will support you with your plan – such as a babysitter one night a week, a carer one day a week who can help with an elderly parent, or problem-solving with your partner how to free up an hour a week so you can work a step towards your bigger vision.

Language can help or hinder

We discovered in Chapter II, Fluid Memory, that language can change what we remember. Language can also affect the likelihood of you sticking to your bigger vision. Psychologists have discovered the power of the words 'don't' and 'can't' when people are faced with temptation. For example, if you've planned to research online courses on writing a winning pitch on Tuesday night when you're home from work, and your best mate rings, asking you out for a drink, what words will increase the likelihood of you successfully resisting the temptation? Studies suggest that if you say 'I can't go' you'll be more likely to give in to temptation and give up the goal you had planned to work towards. You can see it happening: you say, 'I can't. I need to work on my business pitch.' Your mate responds with, 'Oh, come one, one drink won't hurt.'

But if when you're faced with temptation, you use the words 'I don't' you'll be much more inclined to follow through with your goals. So, if when the mate asks you out for a drink, you respond with 'I don't drink on Tuesdays' you'll be much more likely to follow through with your original goal.

Why?

Using the words 'I don't' in response to temptations increases your sense of empowerment with goals, making you more likely to work towards them.

Value in the small steps

We're more likely to work towards a goal in which we can see the value. The steps you've outlined in your five-year plan are for the purpose of bringing your bigger vision to fruition. Reminding yourself of why you're doing the small stuff will help you to achieve the bigger stuff. Novice marathon runners don't decide with one day's notice to run a marathon. They plan, train, begin new behaviours (running distances, interval training, meal planning for races), rest, regroup, replan, train again and race. All of these steps are important to crossing the finish line on the day it matters. All of the steps you've outlined to reach your bigger vision are important to the bigger picture. Reminding yourself of their longer-term value can help keep you going when the going gets tough and you're feeling a pull to give in.

Learning from setbacks

Extraordinary people with or without trauma as a catalyst to success have endured countless setbacks on their road to brilliance. The key is how you respond to setbacks. Use your extraordinary belief to guide extraordinary behaviour in the aftermath of a setback. When the dust settles, ask yourself what the rejected application, flopped interview, unsuccessful business meeting taught you? What can you take away from the event that will strengthen your resolve and improve your capacity for success?

We saw in Chapter II, Fluid Memory, that it can be helpful to update the meaning of unpleasant events: to spot the worst meaning then rewrite it with new information. Linking the updated meaning to the memory of the unpleasant event flattens it, making it less likely to intrude and stir self-doubt. For example, if you performed less than your best in an interview and it leads to rejection, take a moment to spot what you feel it says about you as a person, then update the meaning taking into account your achievements. Re-evaluate the event through the lens of your extraordinary belief, asking, for example, what would someone who is 100 per cent [insert your extraordinary belief – organised, motivated and always achieves their goals when they put their mind to it] learn from this that will strengthen future success?

Know when to try another route

There are times when you hit a setback and realise your success is unlikely to bear fruit on the route you've mapped out. You have to change your route. The key is deciding how many setbacks you're willing to accept before you rethink your direction.

Charlotte is an excellent example of someone who changed her route to bring her bigger vision to fruition. She had dreamed of directing the romantic comedy she had written. With the short film award under her belt, there was no reason to believe that she wouldn't secure funding. And yet she didn't. Meeting after meeting led to promises but no secured investment. Ten years went by. Enough was enough. Charlotte realised she needed to try a different route. She was passionate about bioscience, found a gap in the market, worked out what she would need (a degree) and set about a plan to bring her bioscience company to fruition. Her intention was to create a thriving company and with the profit fund her feature film. She certainly did not reach her bigger vision by the familiar route. But she has reached it.

The message here is know when to change your route. It was tough for Charlotte to leave the film industry. She had a lot of expertise, success and passion in the area as well as a number of years under her belt. But it was absolutely the best thing she did for her bigger vision.

A bout of stress can switch on resilient genes

As you juggle an ever-increasing to-do list with limited amounts of time, you're likely to feel stressed – very stressed if you encounter a setback. Whilst severe stress can cause us to lose track of our longer-term goals, a duel with stress may not be a bad thing. For some people, exposure to stress turns on genes that make them more resilient to future stress. The long-form variant of the gene encoding neuropeptide-Y is one such example.

Neuropeptide-Y (NPY) is a hormone released in the brain during stress, which regulates our physical and emotional reaction to stress exposure. In a study of Special Forces soldiers who faced extreme POW-like stress as part of their military survival training, NPY levels were found to predict better performance during intense interrogation – that is, a better response to extreme stress.

The long-form variant of the gene is related to reduced PTSD after trauma exposure, suggesting that when the gene interacts with adversity (the environment) it promotes resilient responding.

What this means for your track to success is to welcome challenges. They're not a bad thing; they can switch on resilient genes, and you'll likely gain valuable learning that can shape your next steps. Overcoming challenges can increase your grit, your confidence and your capacity to lead.

Aim to be the best

I encourage my clients to plan to achieve one task a day that's linked to bringing their bigger vision to fruition. I encourage one task a day because in my experience, setting the bar at one task a day leads to achieving three a week, which is a lot better than none. In the same vein, aim to be the absolute best, not mediocre, not acceptable, not just-so but the absolute best: aim to deliver the best pitch, offer the best contribution in your meetings, write the best reports for your business, create the best logo for your website, and so on. Aim to be the best and you will be far more than ordinary. You'll be well on the path to extraordinary.

How Charlotte did it

Charlotte faced setback after setback. She was separated from her parents by the age of four, almost died from a severe illness as a teenager, had enormous responsibility heaped on her at too young an age, and dropped out of university with hopes of a better life through marriage only to discover that her husband suffered from alcohol addiction. Charlotte never lost sight of her bigger vision – of having a better life, a life marked by success rather than setback.

Charlotte tapped her *extraordinary belief* in her capacity for success to keep her going, fuelling her strength to apply for a scholarship to an Ivy League university. Here she flourished, *pursuing her passion* in Russian Language and Literature, and, upon graduating, her passion for writing film scripts. After 10 years in the film industry, Charlotte doubted whether she could make it. She *calculated her realistic risk of failure* and determined that based on her life history, the number of goals she had achieved and the few she had not, that her risk of failing was 1 per cent. She *interpreted 'no film funding' as 'try another avenue'*. She applied to the University of Oxford to *pursue another passion*, clinical pharmacology. In her admissions interview, she *put her head together with people who matter* to work out how she might meet the knowledge requirements of the admissions process. She nailed the meeting, impressing the head of department so much they offered her a place on the spot. Charlotte graduated with distinction and started her thriving bioscience company, a company whose profit is funding the production of her romantic comedy.

Charlotte never lost sight of her big vision. She frequently tapped her *extraordinary belief* in her capacity for success, her *image* of succeeding with her adoring grandparents by her side. She tackled self-doubt head-on with statistics, worked out the realistic risk of failing with facts of past success to strengthen her stamina. Charlotte endured adversity in her childhood, which may or may not have switched on resilient genes. She has always, she said, *aimed to be the best* and in this pursuit, she has achieved the extraordinary.

How Can You Take This Forward?

In this chapter, we first covered tools to help you over the start line, then a number of tools to strengthen your stamina to cross the finish line.

Your bigger vision is a lot like running a marathon – it requires planning, often some training, a number of healthy behaviours and tried and tested methods for dealing with self-doubt when you hit a wall. Call on your extraordinary belief wrapped in an image to kick self-doubt and strengthen your stamina.

A worry diary can put your worries into perspective, increasing confidence in your capacity to deal with them and in your knowledge that they rarely come true. Calculating your real risk for failure based on your own achievements will put your potential for success into perspective, spurring you in the right direction.

Like running long distances, your preparation and pace is as important to your persistence as is staying connected to the passion in your bigger picture. Set flexible and realistic expectations. Learn from setbacks and change your route to the finish line if you need to. Put your head together with people who matter to problem-solve. Collaborate.

Intending to take one step, however small, towards your big vision every day will increase the likelihood of you achieving three a week. Remember, finishing a task releases a burst of dopamine, rewarding you for your efforts and progressing you to success. Update memories linked to adversity, if you have them, and be open to the possibility that past bad stuff may have turned on resilient genes.

Finally, aim to be the best, the absolute best, and you will fast progress your path to extraordinary.

In a Nutshell

Motivation gets you started. Determination keeps you going.

To strengthen the motivation to start – take your first step.

Taking your first step unlocks the likelihood that you'll keep going.

A few things make taking the first step easier
- o Bursts of dopamine from achieving small steps
- o The three-minute carrot
- o Break the first step into tiny steps and take the first tiny step
- o Do an average job rather than a perfect job
- o Make sure there's passion and depth in your bigger vision

After the first step
- o Steps that lead to results keep you going. Include a mix of steps in your plan for your big vision that are within your control
- o The just-right challenge. Include stimulating as well as necessary steps in your plan

o Deal with routine decisions the night before
o Deal with opportunities: will this benefit me in some way? Will this take me closer to my big vision?
o Redefine 'no' – it means try another route
o Put your head together with people who matter
o Know what you need and ask for it
o Collaborate
o Balance work with breaks
o Set deadlines, be specific and accountable
o Resist temptations with language: 'I don't' rather than 'I can't'

Dealing with setbacks and self-doubt
o Use a worry diary to discover that almost 90 per cent of your worries won't come true
o Calculate the realistic risk of failing based on the number of goals you've not mastered divided by the number of goals you've set yourself in your whole life x 100%
o A positive thought or image will reduce worry
o Use your extraordinary belief to guide extraordinary behaviour
o Use your winning image to strengthen your confidence
o Set flexible and realistic expectations
o Remind yourself of the value of your bigger picture to keep you going
o Learn from setbacks – what do they teach you that could strengthen your resolve and improve your capacity for success?
o Know when to try another route
o Recognise that adversity can switch on resilient genes and may do for you
o Aim to be the best, the absolute best

VII.

Cultivating Happiness

Many of us have ideas of how winning the lottery would instantly enable us to live an extraordinary life. Whether we imagine travelling the world, starting a charity or snapping up our dream home, we all fantasise that winning a lot of money would transport us out of our current frustrations and challenges and into an extraordinary life.

You may be surprised to learn, however, that most people who win the lottery move back to their original 'set point' of happiness rather quickly. Within a few months, even, they're back to their original level, even though they may have paid off their debt, gone wild with extravagant holidays, invested in new property, quit the job that left them less than stimulated, and bought goodies and gadgets to their heart's content. Why then does their happiness return to pre-winning levels?

It turns out that happiness is not so much about the acquisition of goods or a heaving bank balance, but the attitude we have regarding life, which ebbs and flows over the years and anchors our happiness to a set point. Our set point is affected by many life events, including the losses we face, but more importantly, by how we interpret and handle them.

Creating an extraordinary life is truly a lifetime project. We don't want to wait until the end to enjoy it! So, in this chapter we'll discover how to maximise our happiness on the journey to creating an extraordinary life. We'll learn from Afet who at the age of twenty-four developed an extreme infection after visiting her dentist for a routine check-up. The infection spread through her body, requiring lengthy antibiotic treatment, heart surgery, double amputation and lifelong treatment with blood-thinning drugs. Afet developed PTSD. She recovered with treatment and is now running her own catering business, creating scrumptious delights for clients' special occasions. Afet is a fresh force in the world, a woman overflowing with happiness.

Afet transformed enormous loss on her road through recovery to success. She lost not only her legs and much of her hearing, but also her lifelong dream of having children. Here, we'll learn how she dealt with her losses and the tools she used to return her set point of happiness to its pre-trauma high. We'll also discover how to deal with everyday losses in our own lives and the tools to keep us upbeat and happy on our path to extraordinary success.

Afet's Story

When Afet was twenty-four years old, she had been excited to be studying law and planning a summer wedding. She visited her dentist for a routine check-up and to have her teeth cleaned before her big day. Since Afet had a minor heart condition, she needed antibiotics whenever she had any check-ups or work on her teeth to prevent a possible heart infection. Her dentist cleaned her teeth but forgot to give her antibiotics. Later the same day, Afet fainted. When she came round, she walked to her local ER where she was briefly examined then sent home with headache pills.

The next day was worse: Afet collapsed and did not come round. She was rushed to hospital where the emergency team discovered that they had missed the heart infection she had presented with the day before. When she awoke days later, she was in a hospital bed, nursing staff busy around her. They had performed an emergency tracheotomy to help her breathe and she was on high-dose intravenous antibiotics.

Afet felt excruciating pain in her legs. She described them as looking black and dirty, like they were covered in mud. She wondered if she had been running in a muddy field. Her legs were, in fact, badly infected, having lost circulation due to her heart infection. Afet continued to receive high doses of antibiotics, which led her to lose her hearing, a side effect for some people on such high doses.

The doctors were unable to save her legs and amputated them below the knees. Afet was in hospital for six months, in and out of consciousness while the doctors treated her heart and leg infections. She had multiple surgeries. Much of this time, she was unable to hear the nursing staff since she had lost her hearing, making it impossible to understand what was happening to her. Afet now takes medication every day to keep her blood thin to avoid heart problems and strokes. As a result, becoming pregnant would be fatal.

Afet had walked into hospital after her routine dental check-up. She was determined to walk out. With six months of rehabilitation, Afet did indeed walk out of hospital on prosthetic legs. She had cochlear implant surgery, which restored 60 per cent of her hearing and then began her journey through PTSD.

I treated Afet for PTSD three years after her hospitalisation and within twelve weeks she had fully recovered. She had updated her most frightening memories, focusing on finding ways to reintroduce the meaning of what she had loved about the abilities she had lost and focusing on what she had not lost. Afet pursued her passion in cooking; she retrained, earned a diploma in the culinary arts and launched her cookery website and catering business. Without a doubt, Afet achieved the extraordinary.

1. How to Raise Your Happiness Set Point

Recognising happiness as a choice

We often think happiness is out of our control, that it's based on the circumstances of our lives – our job, where we live, our material possessions, how much money's in the bank, how our boss treats us, the promotions available to us, how often we see our friends, how our partner cares for us, and so on. Or, that we need to achieve a certain degree of success or a certain holiday or even a luxury item like a new car before we'll feel happy. We may feel that happiness is a destination, something that happens once we achieve the big things we're aiming for.

> Happiness, like an attitude, is a mindset we cultivate.

But happiness is a choice, made easier, of course, when we have a lovely boss, lovely cars and homes or a holiday to look forward to. Yet, an encouraging boss, a heaving bank balance, adventurous holiday or a house decked to the brim with our most desired gadgets and luxuries does not guarantee happiness. Happiness, like an attitude, is a mindset we cultivate.

How?

It's worth reminding ourselves of some of the tools we've learned so far, which progress our path to extraordinary, and also boost happiness. We learned in Extraordinary Behaviours that guiding our todays with future-feeling thinking actually helps us to feel happier – making decisions based on how we *want* to feel rather than on how we are feeling.

> Happiness is in the 'doing' and in how we think about what we're doing.

You may hear people say 'I didn't pop into the gym for a workout. Didn't feel like it' or 'I'll start writing my pitch when I'm in a more upbeat mood. I can't write when I'm flat or blue.' Starting a workout or a pitch you've been putting off actually blows away blue feelings because getting started releases dopamine, which makes you feel great. The upbeat feelings reward your efforts and keep you going. They also orientate you towards happier thoughts and memories, and even behaviours, like working through another task on your to-do list or eating a healthy meal after a workout, which kick-starts the next dopamine-reward cycle, all of which increase your likelihood of feeling good.

Happiness is in the 'doing' and in how we think about what we're doing.

When we're feeling happy, it's much easier to get stuff done, to be creative, to problem-solve and to connect with other people. So, when you wake up in the morning, assess how happy you are. Where would you put yourself on a scale of 0 to 10? Where is your set point?

Most British people put themselves at a 7 out of 10 for happiness. Americans start the day at a 6. If you wake up and rate your happiness as a 7, do an experiment: approach your day with an 8. Allow yourself to start your day feeling 8 out of 10 happy. To nudge up one notch on the happiness scale, first thing in the morning, rather than bringing to mind the likely problems you'll be fire-fighting during the day, take a moment to spot three things that are going well right now. These could be small things like the sun is shining, your kids slept through the night, your partner made you coffee, there's little traffic on your route to work, and so on. Find three things that are positive at the start of the day and notice them. Then orientate yourself to thinking and acting like you're 80 per cent happy. How does the world look with an 80 per cent happy lens? What would you do differently throughout the day to keep you feeling 80 per cent happy?

On another day, try moving your happiness set point to 9. Tell yourself, 'Today, I'm going to be 9 out of 10 happy.' Why not? What's stopping you? Increases in happiness and well-being feel great, of course, but there is another benefit. Happy people live longer – on average, by 7.2 years. So . . . orientate your compass to the happy direction. You have nothing to lose. How does this change how you approach your day, the world?

You can also experiment with starting the day with your extraordinary belief, asking yourself: If I 100 per cent believe I'm [insert your extraordinary belief]; for example, I'm a hard-working person who achieves what they put their mind to, a kind person with grit, how would I approach my day differently? Would I let some small stuff slide? And be more inclined to see the bigger picture?

Find your flow with learning

Continuous learning helps to keep the mind sharp, improves memory, can increase confidence and can put you in contact with other people, which also boosts the feel-good factor. In his lifelong studies of thousands of people and their experiences of enjoyment and happiness, psychologist Mihaly Csikszentmihalyi discovered that 15 per cent of the best everyday experiences occur in the context of learning, such as trying a new recipe, a new route to work, a new haircut or more conventional learning endeavours, such as learning a new language or improving your tennis or golf game.

When we learn, we sprout new brain cells, create new neural connections and even increase the volume of specific brain areas. Learning with a balance of challenge and skill can create *flow* – the deeply satisfying experience of full concentration on a specific task during which short-term goals emerge, and which, when achieved, leads to mastering a larger goal. For example, a rock climber hanging off a cliff has the overall goal to reach the summit with short-term goals of finding and securing his next grip, which requires him to approach the task with full concentration, problem-solving in real time. Finding, achieving and solving the challenges en route to the peak is intensely absorbing and rewarding. Flow could also be described as becoming entwined with an activity, fully absorbed in the steps to master the end point. For a chess player, the end point is winning the game and the emergent goals would be each individual move.

So important is learning to happiness that Mihaly describes learning as the pursuit of happiness.

To create flow, we need challenges and we need the appropriate skills to respond to the challenges. When the skills and challenges balance each other, the task usually produces flow.

The more often people report flow-like experiences, the more satisfaction with every aspect of their lives they report and the more involved they are with their work. Of course, not every task is challenging – paying a bill, washing dishes, booking your family's travel, and so on, are far from stimulating endeavours. But add an element of challenge into the mix and you create opportunities for flow. Washing dishes might become 'wash dishes using only two litres of water'. Paying a bill could become 'pay a bill within two minutes'. Book the family's travel plans could become 'book the family's holiday in a part of the country that gives us all an activity we love'.

Adding an element of challenge to your everyday tasks creates opportunities for flow and is likely to boost your happiness levels. For Mihaly, happiness springs from the capacity to find and respond to increasingly complex opportunities, which increases the likelihood for flow and opportunities to build on or learn new skills.

Notice the world outside your head

We saw in Chapter III, Focus, that people feel happiest when they're fully absorbed in something worthwhile and challenging. Throwing your full attention into the tasks at hand will increase happy feelings – especially when you are absorbed in something that is challenging enough to be stimulating, but not so challenging that it's frustrating.

When you focus on a task with your full attention, you're more likely to get absorbed in it, to get lost in it and to find flow, which feels good and is linked to upbeat feelings. You're also more likely to finish the task, which will give a burst of dopamine and . . . a happy feeling.

Noticing what is going on outside your head also helps to increase well-being because it breaks the cycle of repetitive negative thinking. It's hard to dwell on your problems or your worries about the future when you're noticing the wonder in small things – people's kindness, the intricacy of a flower, the challenges a bee faces on his hunt for pollen – noticing the wonder in small things feels good and takes us out of our head and our problems. Moving beyond the perimeter of your mind creates perspective, which instantly reduces worry and rumination, increasing happiness.

So, whenever you find yourself dwelling or worrying, use this awareness as a cue to focus on what you can see and hear right in front of you. Even better, get up and walk outside, take a breath of fresh air. Walk through a park or a woodland. Time in nature helps to reduce stress levels in the brain and in the body. People's heart rates slow down and stress hormones decrease. Being in nature boosts your immunity, most likely because you're benefiting from lower levels of inflammation-inducing stress hormones coursing through your body.

> Seeing the big picture outside your head helps you to return to problems with a clearer mind and punctuates your difficult times with smidgens of happier ones.

If you can't get outside, find the opportunity to look at nature photos. Looking at nature settings has been found to lower levels of anger and aggression, making people feel calm. When you have more than a few moments, do as the Japanese do, go 'forest bathing' – immerse all of your senses in the woods once you're there, noticing what you can see, hear and smell. Take it all in. You're giving your mind a break from decision-making, which is taxing, as well as the demanding focus of work – whether that's office-based or the work linked to maintaining a house or raising a family. As you focus outside your head, you're also observing what is going on rather than using the analytical side of your brain, meaning you'll be less likely to dwell and more likely to feel happy.

Connect with people

Socialising is rated as one of the most positive daily activities, more enjoyable than watching TV or relaxing. We love to socialise and if we make goals that put us into contact with other people, we're more likely to take steps towards those social goals and benefit as a result. A German study asked 1,200 people to rate their life satisfaction and then write a few ideas about how they could improve their life over the next year. People who had made social goals – seeing friends more, volunteering for a charity, helping someone in need – had jumps in life satisfaction within a year, suggesting that connecting with other people makes us feel more fulfilled and happier in the long term.

> A friend who lives within a mile and who becomes happy increases the probability of your happiness by 25 per cent.

Is there a link between the quality of someone's social network and their levels of happiness? To answer this question, James Fowler and Nicholas Christakis studied over 5,000 people and their networks over a twenty-year period. Using sophisticated statistics, they discovered that people who surround themselves with happy people are more likely to be happy, and that happiness spreads. A friend who lives within a mile and who becomes happy increases the probability of your happiness by 25 per cent.

It helps, of course, if you can identify with the people you're connecting with. Psychologists looking at recovery from depression discovered that feeling strong ties or a sense of belonging with the people you're socialising with reduces blue feelings, boosts happy ones and predicts recovery.

The happiest people in the world are highly social. They enjoy stronger romantic and other social relationships than less happy people. The bottom line is – stay in touch with friends, arrange social activities and make some goals that put you in contact with other people. You'll feel happier as a result.

Plan breaks and holidays to look forward to

Throughout this book, we've discovered the benefits of planning our next days as well as our longer-term vision. Planning ahead also works with holidays and is more important to happiness than actually taking them.

In a study of over 1,500 Dutch people, researchers asked about 1,000 of them who were taking a holiday questions about their happiness before and after their vacation. The remaining people were not going on a holiday but still answered questions about their happiness. People about to go on holiday were much happier than people who weren't. But they both reported similar levels of happiness when measured at the point the holidaymakers returned home. Only holidays that were truly relaxing kept people feeling upbeat on return for a short while. The researchers concluded that we're more likely to feel happy with planning and taking many breaks rather than one long stressful holiday. We can also beef up our pre-trip happiness by increasing our anticipation of our holidays – talking about them and planning our trip's activities before we go.

Set goals and achieve them

Goals, big life goals, daily goals or even goals we set ourselves with our everyday chores give opportunities for focus and flow, which increase happiness, as well as bursts of dopamine when we achieve them, strengthening our happiness. Feeling happy motivates what psychologists call goal-directed behaviours – the things we do to successfully reach our goals. And achieving goals fuels greater feelings of happiness.

The more we see the value of a goal and make a task our own, the more we're likely to act towards achieving it. So, try to put your own spin on the goals you give yourself at work and at home, which may be unrelated to your bigger vision, but which help you to achieve the tasks you're expected to achieve on a given day. For example, if you are required to write a report about the impact of your company's website, try to find the thread in the task that could spark a modicum of interest for you – such as choosing your own creative layout for the report, or if this does not spark interest, then setting yourself the goal of writing the draft of the first section in 20 minutes or less. Setting goals for the tasks you absolutely have to achieve yet are only indirectly related to your longer-term vision (in that they, for example, help you earn cash in the short term) will help you achieve them. In so doing, you'll boost your levels of happiness.

Daydream with images of success

In Chapter I, Vision, we learned a lot about the power of positive images. We saw that athletes top up their training with winning imagery, and that positive images have the power to improve how we come across to other people, as well as counteract niggling self-doubts on our path to extraordinary success.

It turns out that imagery, where you imagine yourself pursuing a real-life goal, is linked to well-being and also success in reaching those goals. George Feldman and Carl Dreher asked about 100 college students to note a goal they'd like to achieve within six months. Then they had a third of the students imagine with all five senses achieving their goal including imagining likely obstacles on the path to success and how they would deal with them. They gave other students a muscle relaxation exercise and they gave another third of students no intervention or training. Students completed questionnaires one month later. Only the students who had used imagery to picture reaching their goals made significant progress in achieving them.

Images of success are likely to boost happiness because they make goal-achievement more likely. Positive pictures also break the cycle of repetitive negative thinking, which means less worry and rumination, and more happiness. It's a win-win. So, picture in your mind's eye the image of you reaching your most important goals. You'll be more likely to strive towards them.

Tap your compassion

Compassion rocks when it comes to psychological well-being and happiness. In a study of almost 200 students, Kristin Neff and her team looked at different aspects of compassion for oneself (or self-compassion) and links with positive emotions and qualities. They defined self-compassion as the capacity to extend kindness towards ourselves in instances of pain or failure; the capacity to normalise our difficult experiences by recognising that people around the world have similar struggles, and that our struggles are a part of what she called the larger human experience, and the capacity to see painful thoughts and feelings as passing rather than identifying with them. They discovered that self-compassion was linked to happiness, optimism, positive emotions and qualities such as wisdom, personal initiative, curiosity, agreeableness, extroversion and conscientiousness.

Her team concluded that self-compassion may give rise to happiness because it creates feelings of warmth, connection with others and a sense of balance or equilibrium. When we're happy we're less likely to ruminate or dwell on the past, which is linked to depression. A self-compassionate mindset encourages healthy coping skills and could keep people feeling optimistic about the future. Feelings of compassion for oneself and others activates the left prefrontal cortex, the part of the brain associated with joy and optimism.

Compassion makes you happy and has a host of other benefits, many of which we've touched on in other chapters, in particular Chapter V, Extraordinary Behaviours.

Compassion for other people also increases happiness. A business school professor at Harvard conducted an expensive yet cool experiment where he and his team gave participants $5 or $20 in the morning. Half of the participants were told to spend the money that day on themselves and half were told to spend the money on other people. Participants who had spent the money on other people felt significantly happier than those who had spent the money on themselves irrespective of the amount they received.

Exercise

Exercise reliably boosts the feel-good factor, so much so that it's a recommended treatment for mild and moderate depression. In one study, three groups of patients received a four-month treatment with depression drugs, exercise or both. All three groups benefited with similar improvements in happiness levels but when they were tested six months later, of those taking the depression drugs, 38 per cent had slipped back into depression. The combined treatment group (drugs plus exercise) did a bit better with a 31 per cent relapse rate. By far the best outcome was the exercise-only group. Their rate of relapse was only 8 per cent.

As we saw in Chapter V, Extraordinary Behaviours, exercise helps our muscles clear out harmful depressive chemicals, which may increase the bioavailability of serotonin, boosting happy feelings. The main health benefits of exercise, such as prolonged life and reduced disease risk, come within the first twenty minutes of exercise. So, to glean the benefits of exercise, sweat it out for a minimum of twenty minutes.

Interestingly, a study that came out of Dartmouth College in the US found that people who exercised in the month preceding and on the day of a memory test performed significantly better than people who had sat around the month before the test or who had exercised for the previous month but not on the day of testing or who had a single bout of exercise just on the day of the test. What this tells us is that regular exercise improves our memory as long as we are also exercising on the days we really need to master our memory.

Laugh a lot

Find the funny side in your days. People who laugh a lot enjoy lower blood pressure, improved concentration and lower levels of anxiety, stress and depression. Humour, of the positive kind (not self-deprecating jokes) is linked to mental toughness, meaning that people who laugh a lot or see the funny side in life's obstacles are more resilient to them. Engaging with opportunities to laugh also reduces anxiety and depression. In one study, psychologists gave older people who were living in care homes a once-a-week four-week intervention where they popped in and sang in silly outfits, coaxing the residents to join in with the fun and games. Another group received their usual care. At the end of the four weeks, the older folk who had been a part of silly singing had significantly lower anxiety and depression scores compared to the folk who had no opportunities for such fun.

Intense emotions trigger the sympathetic nervous system, activating the fight–flight response. When the sympathetic nervous system is activated, blood pressure can spike. But humour will keep blood pressure stable in such conditions. This was discovered in a study which asked men to watch a sad movie, a comedy or a dull film. The sad and funny films increased galvanic skin response, which refers to changes in sweat gland activity, indicating activation of the sympathetic nervous system, but only the funny film kept blood pressure stable. The sad film caused blood pressure to spike.

In another study, researchers tricked about fifty students, leading them to believe they would receive an electric shock in twelve minutes. A third of the students listened to a funny audio recording while waiting to receive the shock; a third listened to a dull recording and another third just waited. The researchers didn't actually shock them, but they did measure their anxiety at the end of the wait period. The students who had listened to the funny recording were the only ones whose anxiety decreased whilst anticipating the shock.

It seems that a sense of humour can improve our capacity to deal with stress and to see challenging events, such as electric shocks, as manageable. So where possible, allow yourself to see the lighter side in some of the challenges you may face and laugh out loud. If nothing else, you'll reduce your blood pressure and improve your capacity to deal with future stressors.

Be creative

One of the most reliable ways to kick-start happy feelings is to discover or create something new. It doesn't have to be something ground-breaking like discovering how to solve the problem of cold fusion. It could be discovering a new idea, solving a problem, or pursuing an artistic activity. Creating or discovering new ideas can emerge when you're working intently on a task, a problem arises and you use your resources to solve the problem and keep going. You create a solution.

Mihaly Csikszentmihalyi discovered that what people love most about their favourite activities, such as rock climbing, reading, playing chess, piano, and so on, are the moments during these activities that they're discovering something new – the moments they're being creative.

When we're creative we feel happier. Paul Silvia and his team studied the link between creativity and mood in a large study of students in North Carolina. They took a detailed survey tapping personality traits and the frequency with which they engaged in creative pursuits, such as writing a poem, drawing a picture or making a recipe. The team called the students eight times a day for a week to discover what they were doing and how they felt. When students were caught in the act of creativity, they were much more likely to report feeling happy than when they weren't engaging in creative pursuits.

You don't have to be an artist to benefit from being creative. In a study of almost 700 young adults, Tamlin Conner and her team in New Zealand asked people to keep a diary for two weeks. They had to rate how creative they had been over the course of the day, to describe their overall mood and to rate how much they felt they were flourishing. Tamlin defined creativity as coming up with new ideas, expressing oneself in an original way or spending time in artistic pursuits. People felt happier with a greater sense of flourishing on the days *after* they had been more creative than usual. So, get your creative juices flowing and you'll feel happier as a result.

How Afet did it

Afet taps all of the tools covered in this chapter to add a spring to her step. Early in her physical recovery, Afet realised that *happiness is a choice* – that she could choose to be a happy amputee or to dwell on her losses and repeatedly try to change the past in her mind. She chooses happiness every day, beginning each day by taking a moment to spot at least three things that she's happy about – whether it's the shining sun or that she is free of physical aches and pains.

Afet does not dwell on the past, rather she engages her full attention in solving the many challenges she faces through the day with limited mobility and hearing, which taps her *creativity* and puts her in flow. Afet is deeply engaged in the world around her, she is out of her head, *noticing what is right in front of her* – the marinated onions she's stirring, the stubby carrots she's chopping, the recipes she's creating, her happy clients, the chores at home – she approaches every task with her full focus. Some of the tasks are dull, she says, so she adds a spicy challenge to the mix to transform them into little *learning* adventures, such as learning to balance on one prosthetic leg as she washes up a plate. Afet *connects with other people* every day, seeing her family daily, her friends weekly and her clients a few times a week. Afet continues *to learn*. She achieved a diploma in the culinary arts and is now enrolled in an online course on improving her web presence. Afet *plans and takes breaks* every six weeks or so with friends or family. She *sets goals* and achieves goals linked to most tasks she works on, including the mundane ones. She holds an *image of her success* in mind, a picture of her running her catering business and the joy in her clients' faces when an event comes together. She extends *compassion* to herself when facing tough stuff, such as swimming without her prosthetic legs. Rather than berating herself for looking different, she praises herself for taking the step to exercise. She *exercises* on weekday mornings – she swims. She *laughs a lot.* Afet sees the lighter side to life and appreciates the days that she has rather than mourning the days that are gone.

2. Dealing with Everyday Losses

We all face losses from time to time, some more significant than others, and sometimes even a string of losses – loss of a valuable possession, an enjoyable evening, a promotion or worse, loss of a job or death of a loved one. These everyday losses can knock our happiness in the short term. Here we'll discover how to deal with everyday losses to bump our happiness set point back up to its pre-loss levels.

Loss of a promotion

It's inevitable that we'll face setbacks on our path to extraordinary success. One of the most helpful ways to pick yourself up and dust yourself off is to look at the setback through the eyes of your extraordinary belief, the belief we worked on in Chapter I, Vision. For example, if you were passed over for promotion, rather than slipping into self-defeating thinking, which will make you feel low and trigger stuck-in-a-rut behaviours, ask yourself: what would someone who is 100 per cent [insert your extraordinary belief] do to move forwards? What would their next step be? For example, what would someone who is 100 per cent bright, organised, a problem-solver, a hard worker and a kind person with grit do next to support their success? What would [insert the people who most want you to succeed] suggest you do?

In Chapter II, Fluid Memory, we saw how helpful it is to update the meaning of unpleasant events: to spot the worst meaning then rewrite it with new information. Linking the updated meaning to the memory of the unpleasant event flattens it, making it less likely to intrude and stir up self-doubt. For example, if you were passed over for promotion, you could take a moment to spot what you feel it says about you as a person, then update the meaning taking into account your achievements. Re-evaluate the event through the lens of your extraordinary belief and take it one step further, asking yourself: what would someone who is 100 per cent [insert your extraordinary belief] learn from this that will strengthen their resolve and capacity for future success?

Loss of an enjoyable evening

You're out of the office early, all set to write the budget for your business plan, when your partner reminds you that tonight's the night you're sorting the garage . . . together. (What?! No way! Did you really agree to this? Yep, tonight's the night you're sifting through the stacks of boxes crammed to the brim to find your children's toddler toys for the school's bric-a-brac sale.) You remind your partner that you have to work on your business plan or you'll never get it off the ground in time for the meeting your mate has set up with potential investors. But she doesn't budge. One thing leads to another and you're in the midst of a blazing row. There goes your evening. Even if your partner does agree to sort the garage without you, you're so worked up you doubt you could get much useful budgeting done. What now? How do you save the evening?

We saw in Fluid Memory that many things will affect what we remember, such as how much we've slept, what we're feeling, how we see ourselves and even how a question is phrased. What this means is that when two people go through the same event, their brains create different memories of it. It's safe to say that your sparring partner is going to have a wildly different memory from yours of the blazing row that's ruined your evening.

There's no point dwelling on the incredulous accusations or the fiery thoughts charging your anger. You'll waste time, disrupt your focus and feel downright miserable. It's far better to compromise. If you did agree to a chore, then get stuck in. Once you've made progress on the task you agreed to do, problem-solve how to free up an hour in the next few days to finish up what you had originally planned.

Of course, there are any number of events that can cause our evenings to disappear, such as discovering that your son has left his science project to the last minute and desperately needs your help to start then finish it, your work has saddled you with an urgent deadline for a report on the company's turnover or there is another unexpected event – a child is sick, your pet becomes poorly, your mum rings for advice about your dad who seems to have a really bad memory of late ... Any number of unexpected events can disrupt your plans, your time and your focus.

These disruptions require problem-solving. Many factors affect our capacity to problem-solve but one thing is for sure, we are better problem-solvers when we approach our problems with compassion. So give yourself a break, ask for help, extend the same kindness you extend to your kids or your colleagues to yourself. Solving the evening's disruption or problem with compassion will get your creative juices flowing, which means you'll kick-start some happy feelings in the midst of it all, and guess what? We problem-solve better and get more done when we're happy.

Loss of an opportunity to excel

There will be times when it's just not possible to go the extra mile with your worthy projects or the projects you're leading or contributing to in the office because something's come up somewhere in your life . . . with your children, your partner, your parents or your business. Fear of missing out turns to actually missing out. In this case, it's missing an opportunity to excel, and it's tough. You have to let go of doing something you're really good at which could be really good for your bigger vision. How do you deal with this?

We learned in Chapter IV, Get Out of Your Head with Helpful Thinking Habits, that it's helpful to see decisions as providing different opportunities to explore to be happy. Over time, we make our decisions the right ones by how we think about the outcomes. The decision to let go of an opportunity to excel can become the right decision when we recognise that we've perhaps given ourselves an opportunity to nourish another area of our life. People are happiest when they help others, so recognising that the redirection of your time and energy helps another area of your life will soften feelings of disappointment and stir feelings of compassion, happiness and creativity. When we problem-solve, we tap our creative juices and when we help others, we tap compassion, all of which boost our happiness levels. You will be able to seize the majority of opportunities that come your way. But when you do miss an opportunity to excel in one area of your life, more than likely, you've gained an opportunity to excel in another area.

Loss of meaningful personal possessions

There goes your phone. You had it a minute ago and now you can't find it or your car keys. Are you losing your mind and valuable moments with fretting? Most things we lose day to day (phone, keys) are replaceable. The problem that comes up is that you end up wasting time searching for them or, if they really are gone, replacing them. If you're finding you're misplacing items, slow down. Give yourself extra time and give attention to your routine.

The more we can live our todays with our full attention – our full focus – the less forgetful we'll be. Better attention means better memory, so give your tasks your full focus, including where you put your keys. If things like your phone do go missing, remember what we learned in Get Out of Your Head with Helpful Thinking Habits, avoid catastrophising and instead take steps to solve the problem. Finally, find the humour in the situation. See the lighter side of temporarily losing your gadgets and your marbles. Whilst seeing the lighter side of losing the item, you might just remember where you've put it.

Job loss

Redundancy or other form of job loss can cause significant stress and upheaval. Whilst sometimes redundancy will be the perfect prompt for taking steps towards your big vision, more often than not job loss is an assured way to increase stress and stir self-doubt.

Job loss requires re-planning in the short and long term and it requires reaching out. Whilst it's tempting to withdraw and wallow, reaching out, asking for help, planning your next steps, your finances, running ideas by people, and calling on people in your field are more likely to create opportunities to support your best potential for success.

To inspire next steps, call on your extraordinary belief. Evaluate the event through the eyes of someone who believes they are 100 per cent [insert your extraordinary belief]. Ask yourself: what would someone who is 100 per cent [insert your extraordinary belief] do next? For example, what would someone who is 100 per cent capable, competent, a creative problem-solver and proactive person do next?

Loss of a loved one or a pet we adore

Perhaps the most significant loss to settle is the sudden death of someone or a pet we love. Loss leads to grief and guilt, especially when we wholeheartedly believe we could have prevented their suffering or death. We're likely to equate our emotional suffering with what we think was our loved one's physical suffering at the time of death. Because we're suffering 100 per cent with the loss, we believe that our loved one suffered 100 per cent. Sometimes we feel like they're still suffering.

When we slip into emotional reasoning, we're seeing the world through the lens of our feelings rather than thinking logically. Totally understandable, of course, after such a loss, but emotional reasoning, as we saw in Chapter IV, will keep you stuck in a rut, extending rather than shortening your suffering.

One of the first things I suggest to clients who have lost a loved one and who blame themselves is to write a list of all that they did that was helpful throughout the life of the person or pet who died, and what they did that may have been helpful in the months or weeks before their death. We gradually shift focus away from 'what I could have done' to 'what I did'.

There's nothing more final than death and yet, people who thrive after loss are able to update their loss memory. They link the past to the present to create a sense of continuity rather than a sense of finality. How do they do this? They update their link to loss.

Updating our link to loss

To create a sense of continuity with the memory of someone who has died, we have to spot what they mean to us and what qualities we loved most about them, then we think through what captures the meaning of our loved one or their best qualities today.

An example may help here. One of my clients lost her father suddenly when he suffered a fatal reaction to a standard medical procedure. He had always shielded her from the bad stuff, protecting her from difficulties with her mum and being bullied as a kid. She described her dad as embodying steadfast protection.

We thought through what could capture steadfast protection today. She remembered that her father had planted a tree in her garden months before he died. She said trees symbolised unerring protection for the environment, often outliving humans. When she remembered her father dying, she also recalled all that she had done to help her dad when he was ill. But her memory didn't stop there with the picture of her dad suffering in the hospital bed. She carried the memory forward to a picture in her mind's eye that captured protection, what her dad had represented, captured now in the silver birch tree he had planted in their garden.

When we deeply love another person, we know them well, they have become a part of us. We know what they'll say when we're late home from work or if we have a dilemma we need to chat through. One of the things we may miss most about losing the people we love are our conversations, the closeness, the simpatico we shared when we talked through events, trivial and traumatic.

Whilst we cannot physically bring back the person who died, we can take a moment to imagine them in a comfy setting where we enjoyed ourselves. Whilst imagining them, we can chat with them in our mind's eye, saying what we may need to say, things that perhaps we did not have a chance to say whilst they were alive. We know how they'll respond, what words they'll say to us. We can imagine this in our mind's eye, or we may want to write about it.

We update our loss, which is no longer focused on 'this person is no longer here', but rather 'how can I take this person with me?' We take the meaning of the person forward as my client did. We can also imagine our loved one at peace, no longer suffering, having a frank chat about the trivial and more difficult stuff we face, encouraging us a little or a lot. We link the past to the present to create a sense of continuity rather than finality and in this way, we change our relationship to loss.

What about gritty loss images?

There are times in our lives when we'll be overcome with images in our mind of people or pets we have loved who have died. This is a normal part of early grief and the images become less frequent over time. But an image of loss can pop to mind years after the death of a loved one. If this happens, you can try to run the image on to a picture in your mind's eye that captures the meaning of the person who died or to an image of them no longer suffering.

To create an image that captures the meaning of your loved one, we first spot what the person means to you and then what may represent this meaning today. You may remember Joshua from Chapter II, Fluid Memory. When he was deployed to Iraq for the first time, handing out toys, clothing and supplies on a humanitarian aid mission, he was shot in a sniper attack with his close friend, staff sergeant Marlin Harpur. A 50-calibre bullet instantly killed Harpur and landed in Joshua's right leg.

Harpur had been a tower of strength, boosting morale and vitalising the whole platoon. His death was a huge loss to the soldiers. A principled and solid man, he led his platoon through the rough and rocky challenges of combat. For Joshua, Harpur captured compassion, courage and strength. Joshua carried what Harpur meant to him forward in the work he chose after his injury. He made it his mission to instil strength in soldiers who had been roughed up and shaken by active duty. When he had images of Harpur lying next to him with wounds in his heart, he fast-forwarded the image to a picture in his mind's eye that captured compassion, courage and strength – a picture of soldiers he had helped overcome emotional injuries linked to combat. In this way, he transformed gritty images of Harpur's death, and he carried the meaning of him into his future.

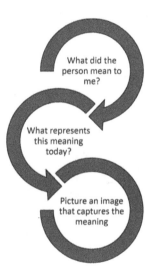

The questions to answer to help you transform images of the loss of a loved one are: what did the person mean to me? What represents this meaning today?

Once you've spotted the meaning and what captures it today, practise running the image on. What this means is that when the painful image comes to mind, take a moment to transform it into an image that captures the meaning of your loved one or an image that shows they are no longer suffering.

You may want to call to mind an image that represents the meaning of your loved one like Joshua did. Or, you may want to call to mind an image that shows your loved one is no longer suffering, such as picturing them in the caring company of loved ones who have passed away or perhaps you may picture them in a place where you enjoyed time together or a spiritual place. Some people find it comforting to picture their loved one at peace next to them. Experiment with what works best for you. And remember to find comfort in your extraordinary image for success, which may or may not include an encouraging picture in your mind's eye of your loved one who passed away. Remember, Sir Ranulph Fiennes' extraordinary image includes two people he loved who had passed away: his father and grandfather.

How did Afet do it?

Afet suffered significant loss: loss of her legs, 40 per cent of her hearing and loss of her capacity to have children. One of the worst moments of her life was the moment the consultant surgeon told her he would have to amputate her legs. Afet had flashbacks to this moment and remembered thinking at the time that her life was over. She struggled to update this memory. To help her memory of this moment become more fluid, rather than stuck, we looked at the worst meaning of losing her legs. She believed that losing her legs meant that her life was over, that she would be bedbound or in a wheel-chair for ever, and that she was no longer a woman.

Afet gradually shifted her thinking from focusing on what she had lost to spotting what she was still able to do. She could still use her sharp mind. She could still walk, albeit with prosthetic legs and much more slowly. She could still feel love and enjoy her family and friends. She could no longer jog to keep fit, but she could swim. She could pursue her many passions, her primary one being cooking. She could still bring joy to the people around her.

With a little help from me, but not much, she updated her worst moment to: 'At the time, I thought that my life was over and that I'd need a wheelchair for the rest of my days. Walking again seemed like an impossibility. The reality, however, was that whilst my life *had* changed, it was far from over. It just meant that I would need to learn new skills like walking, sitting down, standing, even rolling over in bed. I was not bedbound, and I do use a wheelchair now, but only as a computer chair! I walk with the help of prosthetic legs and I walk more slowly but I do walk. I am proud of how far I've come. Whilst life will never be the same again, I have achieved a lot and I am walking proof that there is indeed life after amputation.'

Whenever the memory of the surgeon came to mind, Afet reminded herself of what she knows now and of what she has not lost.

Afet also spotted what being a woman meant to her. She said it meant being feminine, having varied roles and being strong, as well as wearing nice clothes and high heels, being bright, caring, energetic and motherly. Afet could not wear high heels, but she could wear stylish clothes, make-up and her favourite perfume. She could no longer wear stiletto heels, but she could walk safely in heels that were two inches in height. Afet recognised that she was bright, caring and energetic and that she had similar values to other women.

Afet had dreamed of having children. She was no longer able to as a result of the lifelong medications she needed. We looked at what it meant to be a mother and what she had been looking forward to in having biological children, and how she may be able to find new ways to create a similar meaning in her life today.

Afet said that motherhood was about loving and nurturing a small being. She was less attached to the idea of a toddler and a teenager. I asked Afet to think how she could introduce something to love and nurture into her life today. Could she love and nurture one of the many babies already in the world who needs a loving and caring parent? Could she love and nurture a project that is important to her? Afet chose two ways to bring the meaning of motherhood into her life: she chose to nurture her passion in the culinary arts and she chose to rescue a kitten, a little being she could love and nurture.

Afet transformed enormous loss on her path to extraordinary success. She worked hard to spot the meaning of her losses and to update them. She found new ways to experience the meaning of being a woman and of motherhood, new ways of bringing this meaning into her life today.

How Can You Take This forward?

Recognise that happiness is a choice. We can nudge our happiness set point up a notch with the tools we've covered in this chapter.

To tip your compass to the happy direction begin your days noticing three things that you're happy about, including the small things like that the sun has briefly poked out from behind the clouds. Get out of your head as much as possible to notice the world around you, and to interrupt unhelpful thinking cycles like dwelling or worry. Socialise! It's one of the most highly rated daily activities.

Create opportunities for flow by adding a challenge to your chores, such as giving yourself a time limit for paying a bill, washing the dishes and so on. Plan holidays and beef up your anticipation by talking about them before you go. Set goals and, importantly, achieve them. Calling to mind images of you achieving your goals increases your success with them.

Extend kindness to yourself as well as to other people and get sweaty twenty minutes a day. That's all it takes to glean the benefits of exercise for your mood and your brain. Laugh, see the lighter side in your struggles and be creative, even if this means creatively washing your dishes. When our creative juices flow, we feel a lot happier and enjoy a sense of flourishing.

Deal with your losses, the big and the little ones. Call on your extraordinary belief, it will guide you through unpleasant events like the loss of a promotion or a job. Some losses, like the loss of an enjoyable evening or an opportunity to excel, do better with a compassionate brain or with humour, both of which boost the happiness factor.

Big losses are hugely painful. When the dust settles, spot what the lost person or pet in your life means to you. Create a continuous connection to the positive meaning of what you have lost, discovering ways to bring the meaning of the person or pet into your life today. This helps you to come to terms with loss and to prepare for the next steps: cultivating happiness.

In a Nutshell

Our happiness ebbs and flows over the years around a set point. How we see and handle life events and losses can affect our happiness set point.

Happiness, like an attitude, is a mindset we cultivate.

Eleven tips for raising your happiness set point
1. Recognise happiness as a choice
   o Experiment with moving your happiness set point up a notch
   o Start your days noticing three things that are going well or beginning your day through the lens of your extraordinary belief
   o Make decisions to get active based on how you want to feel rather than on how you are feeling
2. Find your flow with learning
   o Add a challenge to your tasks
3. Notice the world outside your head
   o Give your tasks your full attention
   o Walk through a park or woodland
   o Look at nature photos
4. Connect with people
   o Socialise
5. Plan breaks and holidays to look forward to
   o Talk about them before you go
6. Set goals, even little ones, and achieve them
   o Put your own spin on the goals you give yourself at work and at home
7. Daydream with images of success
   o Picture success and see yourself overcoming obstacles

8. Tap compassion
   o For yourself and others
9. Exercise
   o Twenty minutes is all that's needed
10. Laugh a lot
   o See the lighter side in some of the challenges you face
11. Let your creativity flow
   o Come up with new ideas, express yourself in an original way or try an arty activity like painting or woodwork

Transform Losses

- Call on your extraordinary belief to guide you through the loss of a promotion or job
- Tap compassion to problem-solve better the loss of an enjoyable evening or an opportunity to excel and see the lighter side in these frustrations
- Spot the meaning of a loved one who has passed away and discover ways to bring the meaning into your life today
- Fast-forward painful loss images to images that represent the best meaning of your loved one or picture your loved one no longer suffering

VIII.

Conclusion

Discovering why some people can overcome adversity or trauma and lead extraordinary lives while others crumple in the same circumstances is the question that has driven much of my scientific research over the years. We know we will face setbacks and, at times, difficult circumstances in our lives. It is often during our difficult times that we step back and re-evaluate our lives, making choices to recreate better futures. This book was inspired by the idea that we can create more fulfilling futures without waiting for the difficult times to kick-start a new perspective or change. We can be extraordinary now.

There is enormous hardship in the world. Some people will live through horrendous trauma. How they recover and thrive has great capacity to teach us how to thrive in our own lives while simultaneously honouring their stories and what they have achieved.

I have long been fascinated in figuring out what can be extrapolated from people's successes in overcoming trauma and applied to anyone's journey, regardless of whether or not they experience a trauma. As a psychologist, I am passionate about reducing people's suffering and guiding them through recovery to reclaim and rebuild their lives. I am regularly blown away by my clients' capacity to run well beyond their recovery to lead lives that match their dreams rather than their fears. I see transformations daily and am grateful to be a part of people's initial steps towards creating recovery and success.

As a scientist, I am intrigued by patterns of human behaviour and am especially interested in the exceptions to these patterns. These exceptions teach us a lot about what it takes to transition from ordinary to extraordinary and the tools to support this process. In my research, I have distilled these processes, evaluated them and created methods for tuning them to our own lives so that we all may benefit.

In *Be Extraordinary* I have attempted to pull all of the processes together in one place and share them in an easily accessible format with real-life examples of how ordinary people have accessed them on their paths to success.

Part of my work as a psychologist is to guide people to recover from PTSD. I often go one step further, working with people to tap their full potential. Every day we have the opportunity to make choices that will take us in the direction of creating extraordinary lives and using our full potential. My clients have taught me that time is limited. Our todays may not be our tomorrows. Why wait to lead an extraordinary life in the future, when you can start creating yours now?

Every process in this book has its place in the transformation of ordinary to extraordinary. We need a *vision* for our lives, and we need to transform niggling self-doubts and limiting images to have the confidence to reach our goals and a plan to take us there. Extraordinary beliefs nestled within your winning images help guide extraordinary behaviours and encourage you to pick yourself up and dust yourself off when you hit a setback on your path to success. We must master our memories to master our future, and *fluid memory* is the key to keeping our memories rich and fluid rather than disorganised and stuck. *Focused attention* will ensure you bring your worthy projects to fruition sooner rather than later and will help you to feel more confident as you focus more on the here and now rather than on feelings of fear, failure or doubt. Getting out of your head with *helpful thinking* will stop dwelling in its tracks and lead you to feel happier whilst thinking more clearly. *Extraordinary behaviours* will ensure you banish avoidance for good whilst paving your path to success with healthy behaviours. Whilst motivation will get you started, it is *determination* that will keep you going to reach your full potential and your bigger vision. *Cultivating happiness* will help you to transform losses and choose happiness daily so you feel more upbeat, on top of your life, can think more clearly and get more done. All of these processes are needed to create and sustain an extraordinary life.

What struck me as I was writing *Be Extraordinary* was discovering that some tools support many processes within the Be Extraordinary framework. These were planning ahead, compassion and proactive language. Planning ahead as a tool for success came up in Vision as a method for planning an extraordinary future. We also saw planning ahead was linked to the process, Focus, since planning your tomorrows in chunks facilitates greater focus when the time comes. Planning ahead was one of the Extraordinary Behaviours, reliably improving well-being on the path to success. We also saw planning ahead in Determination as a tool for dealing with decisions – plan to deal with routine decisions the night before to free up time and brain power for dealing with tough decisions the next day. Planning ahead again came up in Cultivating Happiness – as a method for boosting the feel-good factor, specifically by planning holidays. It's the planning of holidays that boosts happy feelings more so than taking the holidays themselves.

Compassion was the next tool linked to the processes that drive an extraordinary life that appeared throughout the book. In Vision, we discovered that creating an extraordinary belief as well as an extraordinary image is best done by including people in the belief and in the image who most want us to succeed. In moments of doubt or setbacks, calling to mind the belief or image of the people who care about us and who most want us to succeed helps us to tap compassion for ourselves and to think more clearly. Compassion came up in Fluid Memory for dealing with blazing rows. We learned that our sparring partner will have a different memory of testy arguments and that we're best off taking a break, which helps us to tap compassion, leading to swifter problem-solving of the issues that cause us to clash. We saw in Focus that compassion can help us to start overwhelming tasks by reducing stress hormones. We saw that a compassionate mindset was one of the Extraordinary Behaviours that lowers stress hormones and improves problem-solving. We also saw in Determination that compassion helps us to deal with self-doubt when we call to mind our extraordinary image, which includes the kind faces of the people who most want us to succeed. Finally, we learned a lot about compassion in Cultivating Happiness, discovering that it's linked to happy feelings and activation of the left prefrontal cortex, which drives optimism and joy.

The power of language touched many processes linked to becoming extraordinary. We saw in Get Out of Your Head with Helpful Thinking Habits that proactive language defines extraordinary thinking. We saw in Determination that we're more likely to resist temptations when we use specific language: 'I don't' versus 'I can't'. We saw in Vision that language is critical to the beliefs we form about ourselves. And we saw in Fluid Memory that language, a juicy or a dry word, can change a memory, which can help or hinder us.

The path to extraordinary success taps all of the processes described in *Be Extraordinary*. My hope for you is that you will use this book in an active way to bring the content alive and take action towards an extraordinary life.

Share your success stories with friends, colleagues, on social media and our website, so that your achievements ripple outwards, inspiring the people close to you and further afield.

The world benefits from extraordinary people. Tap your full potential. Be Extraordinary.

Useful Resources

This book is about becoming extraordinary without suffering trauma as a catalyst. It is aimed at people who may or may not have experienced some setbacks in their life rather than people who have suffered significant trauma and have post-traumatic stress disorder (PTSD). Whilst the tools in this book are helpful for some symptoms of PTSD, it is not a treatment for PTSD. The most effective treatment for PTSD is short-term trauma-focused cognitive behavioural therapy.

The following website provides more information on PTSD: www.transformtrauma.co.uk

On the Online Register for CBT for the UK and Ireland, you can access qualified therapists who treat PTSD: http://www.cbtregisteruk.com/

The NHS Improving Access to Psychological Therapies Programme (IAPT) offers government-funded treatment for anxiety disorders and depression. Most IAPT services allow you to self-refer. Simply enter your postcode into the following website to locate your closest IAPT service and to determine whether or not you may self-refer or require a GP referral to access the service. https://www.nhs.uk/Service-Search/Psychological-therapies-(IAPT)/LocationSearch/10008

The *Complete CBT Guide for Anxiety*, part of the Overcoming series, includes a chapter on Post-traumatic Stress Disorder, which shows you how to determine whether or not you are suffering from PTSD and what to expect in your CBT treatment.

Wild, J. & Ehlers, A. (2013), 'Post-traumatic Stress Disorder' in R. Shafran, L. Brosnan, and P. Cooper (Eds), *The Complete CBT Guide for Anxiety*. Robinson, London: 2015

Herbert, C., *Overcoming Traumatic Stress, 2nd Edition: A Self-Help Guide Using Cognitive Behavioural Techniques*. Robinson, London: 2017

Wetmore, Ann, *An Introduction to Coping with Post-Traumatic Stress, 2nd Edition*. Robinson, London: 2019

Acknowledgements

A number of people have made *Be Extraordinary* possible. First and foremost, I would like to thank Andrew McAleer at Little, Brown for keenly supporting the book and for his careful reading of the manuscript. I'd also like to thank Andrew for editing the original title to *Be Extraordinary*.

I'd like to thank my mentors and colleagues with whom I have had the privilege to work for almost twenty years: Anke Ehlers and David M. Clark. My work with Anke and David and their team has shaped my thinking and my research and clinical practice, and I am grateful. I would like to thank Amy Sedgwick, whose positivity and practical attitude helped me to reach the finish line, and for her valuable comments on many of the chapters. I would like to thank my dearest friends, Sandra Moon Dancer, Jenifer Brenner, Mubeen Rowe, Olivia Merriman-Khanna, Michelle Moulds, Anne Morizon, Georgina Tan, Tanya Son and Kaj Espen Nyland, for making me laugh out loud and often over the years.

I'd like to thank my family for exemplifying many of the skills in this book: Patricia Minden, who also offered the just-right mix of grit and encouragement, an incredible life story, enriching education and a fountain of support; my dear sister, Allison Wild, who gave the most helpful feedback on the proposal, the pitch and the cover design, I value you always; my brothers, Anthony Wild and

Alexander Wild, and my father, James Wild, who have inspired with their own life stories.

I'd like to extend my heartfelt thanks to Sylvia Toskan, Shirley Russ and Georgina Eckardt, whose unconditional kindness is with me always. I'd like to thank Gabriella Tyson, who helped to redraw the cycles in Chapter IV, and the artist Juni Bøe Nyland, who drew original images at short notice. I'd like to thank my godchildren, Harmony Rump Jagla and Konrad Rump Jagla, for offering fun breaks and fresh perspectives.

I would like to thank the seven contributors to *Be Extraordinary*: Kenny, Joshua, Mary, Joyce, Caroline, Charlotte and Afet. Your stories are extraordinary. I would like to thank my copy-editors, Rebecca Sheppard and Alison Tulett, for making the copy-edit process effortless. Finally, I would like to thank my writing companions, Sami, Pip and Zak, and the memory of Joey, who will for ever and always run with me.

Index